Reality
Transformed

Reality Transformed

Film as Meaning and Technique

Irving Singer

The MIT Press
Cambridge, Massachusetts
London, England

This book was set in Palatino by Wellington Graphics.

Printed and bound in the United States of America.

Library of Congress Cataloging-in-Publication Data

Singer, Irving.
    Reality transformed : film as meaning and technique / Irving Singer.
        p. cm.
    Includes bibliographical references and index.
    ISBN 0-262-19403-1 (hc. : alk. paper)
    1. Film criticism—Philosophy. I. Title.
PN1995.S513 1998
791.43′01—dc21   98-17339
                                                                              CIP

To Mark

·

Contents

Books by Irving Singer

Reality Transformed: Film as Meaning and Technique

Meaning in Life:
The Creation of Value
The Pursuit of Love
The Harmony of Nature and Spirit

The Nature of Love:
Plato to Luther
Courtly and Romantic
The Modern World

Mozart and Beethoven: The Concept of Love in Their Operas

The Goals of Human Sexuality

Santayana's Aesthetics

Essays in Literary Criticism by George Santayana (editor)

The Nature and Pursuit of Love: The Philosophy of Irving Singer
(edited by David Goichoechea)

Preface

This book should be read as an extended essay. It does not pretend to be a comprehensive treatment of film theory or aesthetics. It is not written as a survey of all the problems in these fields; it is not a guide to the work, much of it excellent, that others have done in the recent decades since film studies became reputable in academic circles; and it does not attempt to reach final or resounding conclusions about the various issues it discusses. Instead of undertaking an exhaustive treatise, I have wanted to articulate a philosophical perspective that some may find unneeded but others can possibly use to stimulate their own critical ideas about presuppositions that have already become habitual and even encrusted in the profession.

In developing my general theme, I have referred to other people's writings only when they abutted my own or else lay across my path as worthy specimens of thinking I find dubious in some respect. As the reader will immediately perceive, my formulations often originate as a response to these contrary views. They have enabled me to recognize problems in this area of investigation that lend themselves to a different approach, and they have forced me to reconsider theoretical assumptions that grew in me throughout the years without my seeing how greatly they required clarification. I am much indebted to the sources I have criticized in my attempt to further whatever line of speculation I was pursuing at the moment. I apologize to others whose writings I have neglected: they did not have that self-serving utility for me.

My thesis in this work is very simple, and it may well appear outmoded to those who prefer the methodologies of science rather than the impressionistic mentality that has generally characterized the humanities. I accept that mentality as a basis for discerning what is fundamental in the nature of film. I believe that all art, and cinematic art in particular, is best understood as life-enhancement, and that when we study it for its human import or philosophic scope, as well as for its use of specialized technology, we find that the meanings and techniques in each work are internally related to one another. The meanings in a film emanate from the cinematic devices that comprise the diversified nature of the medium. But that itself exists only as a way of expressing and exploring problems that matter to human beings, problems they care about and have to face throughout their lives. Investigation of these problems, both cognitive and affective, is the province of humanistic philosophy and literary studies in general.

My essay tries to show how these disciplines can have a harmonizing relevance to a visual art of the sort that film is. Harmonization being my goal, I use it in an attempt to move beyond the persisting controversies between realists and formalists in film theory. I mingle elements of both approaches in my idea that film is not inherently a re-presenting or recording of reality but rather a pictorial and usually narrative transformation of it. In developing this suggestion, and above all in my treatment of the movies I analyze, I emphasize that reality as portrayed in films is always a product of formalist techniques and creative innovations that enable some filmmaker to express what he or she considers real in the apparent world.

Part I of this work deals with the philosophical dichotomy between appearance and reality that has affected a great deal of film theory in the twentieth century. With transformation as my guiding principle, I then analyze Woody Allen's *The Purple Rose of Cairo*, a film whose thematic content raises questions about appearance and reality and their relation to film as a whole. In part II I examine theories that have taken the fact that film is a visual art to be sufficient justification for subordinating its literary components. Here again, I map out an approach that seeks to harmonize opposing points of view. I argue that film transforms our visual perception of reality through concepts that are basically literary and dramatic. I inspect Luchino Visconti's *Death in Venice* to show how a filmmaker's excessive fidelity to the visual can impair his use of conceptual elements he has derived from his literary source.

Part III and the conclusion draw together various strands in the previous chapters by studying questions about film as a mode of communication that must nevertheless cope with our alienation from the realities being transformed through the very techniques that give them meaning in this art form. Jean Renoir's *The Rules of the Game* is instructive here. It reveals how, within the texture of a dramatic comedy, a filmmaker can present transformations that not only harmonize appearance and reality and the visual and the literary but also surmount the antithesis between communication and alienation.

The transformational versatility of *The Rules of the Game* consists in its dialectic of ambiguities and uncertainties about the human condition, in contrast to any dogmatic or grossly definitive solutions. That seems to me the proper ambience for a work of art, and also for essays in philosophy. It is the perspective that I have tried to elaborate throughout this book.

I am indebted to many people, including my students in different courses at MIT, for encouraging me to think that my ideas about film might be worth writing out and being read. For help and useful comments at different stages of the manuscript, I am particularly grateful to Richard Allen, George Bluestone, Noël Carroll, Gail Finney, Henry Jenkins, Richard A. Macksey, Miles Morgan, David Perkins, Ben Singer, Jo Singer, Katherine Stern, Yuri Tsivian, Ralph Wedgwood, and Richard Wilbur.

I. S.

Introduction: Realism vs. Formalism

Classical film theorists are often divided into two types: the formalists and the realists. In the first camp are Sergei Eisenstein, Rudolf Arnheim, Béla Balázs, and many others; in the second, Siegfried Kracauer, André Bazin, and their followers. While the realists emphasize that film records properties of the physical world that lend themselves to the photographic process, the formalists call attention to the technical means by which a filmmaker goes beyond the real world in order to express his or her artistic vision. The differences between these two ways of approaching film have led to acrimonious debates, and it would be foolish to pretend that they can easily be quieted. Arnheim's formalist claim that the realism of sound jeopardizes the aesthetic integrity achieved by the best of the silent films would seem to be worlds apart from Bazin's belief that sound, like deep-focus shots, is authentically cinematic *because* it enables us to duplicate reality most completely. Formalists and realists differ in their ideas about symbolism, dream effects, cutting, editing, choice of subject matter, and in general the nature of a filmmaker's inventiveness.[1]

In relation to all such questions, the ensuing controversies can have far-reaching importance for creative practice as well as theory, and for criticism as well as the responsiveness of ordinary moviegoers. Nevertheless, it may be possible to step back from the conflict and to cut across the divisions that separate the warring camps. By looking at film from a point of view that both sides share though fail to accentuate, perhaps we can find a means of harmonizing their divergent attitudes. In the history of ideas this has been a service that philosophers have often provided, albeit with varying success.

Several theorists, notably Jean Mitry and Noël Carroll, have taken steps in this direction.[2] I will seek to provide further suggestions from my own point of view. In the last twenty or thirty years professionals in the field of cinema studies have tended to ignore the ongoing differences between realists and formalists. That debate seemed to have reached a stalemate, and academic interest veered toward the possibility that one or another of the current developments in linguistics or political philosophy or psychoanalytic theory might be more productive for the making of generalizations in film ontology and aesthetics. In a book he co-edits with Noël Carroll, David Bordwell has recently portrayed this interlude as a quest for what he calls a "Grand Theory." He also refers to it as "the Theory," in contrast to less ambitious theorizing about the many aspects of film production and experience that comprise the nature of this art form.[3]

Limiting themselves to the movements that have been most influential in the last three decades, Bordwell and Carroll describe the Theory as "an aggregate of doctrines derived from Lacanian psychoanalysis, Structuralist semiotics, Post-Structuralist literary theory, and variants of Althusserian Marxism. . . . The Theory was put forth as the indispensable frame of reference for understanding all filmic phenomena: the activities of the film spectator, the construction of the film text, the social and political functions of cinema, and the development of film technology and the industry."[4]

Bordwell, Carroll, and most of those they include in their anthology are aware that different adherents to the Theory emphasize different modes of thinking that must be addressed individually. There is no need for me to duplicate this concerted attack upon the multiple heads of the dominant hydra. The newer approach intrigues me in two respects. I applaud its inherent anti-essentialism, but as yet I am not convinced that its piecemeal method of analysis is adequate for dealing with many of the fundamental problems that the Theory, or rather the rival Theories, tendentiously dismissed.

Carroll, in particular, recognizes most acutely that there is no one definition or avenue of thought that can fully account for everything that is ordinarily referred to as film or cinema or the art of motion pictures. His posture is therefore empirical, even nominalistic on occasion. He substitutes minute and careful analysis for the grandiloquence of metaphysical speculation. That is a fine beginning for a healthy philosophy of film. I note, however, that except in some limited discussions neither he nor his compatriots come to grips with all the underlying questions that the classical realists and formalists raised and that the subsequent Grand Theorists swept aside as retrograde to the universal dogmas asserted in their linguistic or Marxist or psychoanalytic pronouncements.

In studying the philosophical bases of both realism and formalism, I revert to the pluralistic approach I defend in other areas of aesthetics and the theory of value. The Grand Theory ideas that are now being eroded do not lead to the flexible and harmonizing syntheses that pluralism provides throughout. Turning away from the quarrel between realism and formalism, the Theories generally incorporated some version of either one or the other. But it was usually presented with little clarity and less than sufficient concern about alternate views equally worth considering.

In my attempt to rectify this situation, I employ a notion that the formalists relied upon more often than the realists—the concept of transformation. Thinkers like Eisenstein, Arnheim, and Balázs argue that film becomes an art by *transforming* what is real instead of merely reproducing or recording it. Since they identify reproduction with indiscriminate photography, the formalists stress the role of technical maneuvers that alter reality for the sake of aesthetic creativity. At the same time, these formalists are aware that film "captures" reality, in one sense or another. Like many of the realists, they think of film as an opportunity to express attitudes about the world, to articulate visual metaphors relevant to the human condition, and even to assert ideological beliefs.

Eisenstein and Balázs are especially alert to the socio-political implications present throughout the making of films. Like some formalists in the theory of painting, Roger Fry and Clive Bell for instance, they sometimes claim that cinematic art can penetrate to transcendental truths accessible only by artistic techniques that go beyond, not copy, whatever appears in ordinary experience. Their formalist insights are not limited to details about the camera or trick photography.

At the same time, formalists tend to neglect the extent to which the photographic images in film resemble empirical reality and are sometimes experienced as if they *were* that reality. Realists emphasize the importance of this element of film ontology. But in focusing on it, the realists lumped together ideas of recording, reproducing, duplicating, and representing without analyzing the disparate ways in which each transforms reality and thus does more than merely capture it.

To formulate a theory that can use elements of both realism and formalism, we must recognize that cinematic transformations arise from human and organic aptitudes that have a constitutive, not just causal, role in the making of movies. In ways that are often unique to itself, film satisfies needs, affective as well as cognitive, that are ingrained throughout our species. These needs are basically the same as those that motivate us in everyday life. But like our view of reality, they, too, undergo transformation by the film experience. They are processed by artificial constructions, in the manner of all artistic expressiveness, and are frequently made more manageable, sometimes more gratifiable, than they might have been otherwise.

These humanistic intimations will serve as a touch-
stone for the theory of transformation I develop
progressively in each chapter. I think the formalists
misconstrued this phenomenon because, despite their
insights into the creativity that makes film an art form,
they misunderstood how transformation furthers communication among human beings. The transformations
that belong to film must therefore be reanalyzed. In
being a vehicle of communication, film changes reality
through techniques that matter because of meanings
they are able to generate. Though the possibility of
metaphysical import need not be ruled out, the meaningfulness that joins a filmmaker to his or her audience
is coherent with their mutual attempts to deal with daily
problems in life. To the extent that film has a "language"
of its own, it systematically transforms realities internal
or external to ourselves, and does so in order to purvey
novel perspectives upon those realities.

In recent decades semioticians have carefully inves-
tigated the language of film, but they often underplay
the human context in which cinematic communication
occurs. It combines different motives: our typical desire
to realize and express feelings we experience as
individual participants in nature, to share with others
the varied responses that demonstrate what we are, to
present ideas about the world, to create a general vision
that people like ourselves can find meaningful, to
establish our identity as human beings living within
traditions that embody cultural and emotional potenti-
alities of our species, to resolve interpersonal difficulties
that all men and women face, and to struggle with

economic, political, and psychological problems that have made it so hard for humankind to cooperate in a search for communal harmony.

Films transform reality by exploring imaginative possibilities of communication in these diverse areas of life. The mere inclusion of realistic images would be useless for anything that massive. Nor can it be explained by reference to the technical procedures that most formalists study as their professional expertise. The communication present in cinematic art originates with a filmmaker who perceives reality through technological devices that are suitable for conveying whatever ideas and feelings he or she wishes to express. In the act of expression, reality is creatively transformed.

For their part, classical realists such as Kracauer or Bazin—to say nothing of neorealists like Cesare Zavattini and Roberto Rossellini—also understand that films are not just reproductions. Though they believe that photographic images are ontologically fundamental in film, they recognize the moral and social impact that can result from photography's ability to display what is factual in our existence. This aspect of the realist position, above all in the sensitive writing that distinguishes Bazin's film criticism, encourages me to think that much of realism can be encompassed within the harmonizing approach I am now suggesting. Reality may be revealed through photographic images, but, as I will argue, the *use* of these images shows the extent to which reality has been transformed. The transformational function makes it possible for a filmmaker to communicate effectively with an audience that has learned how to experience cinematic art.

Though I propose the notion of transformation as a means of reconstructing formalist and realist theories, I do not wish to deny that their manifestos and official utterances sometimes introduce polemical theses that may well be irreconcilable. Disagreements of that sort frequently arise from philosophical dilemmas that lie below the surface of art theory. In this book I will concentrate on three of these residual issues. Each is important for appreciating both the content and the nature of the films I will be discussing in terms of them. Works of art are often reflexive inasmuch as they have components that are pertinent not only to the character of their medium but also to their own formal and referential structure. My critical analyses of the three movies I have chosen seek to elucidate their employment of philosophical themes as well as the relevance of these themes for a theory of cinematic art as a whole. Without engaging every problem in ontology or aesthetics, we may be able to lay the groundwork of a general philosophy of film.

As a brief foretaste of the governing concepts in this venture, it will be helpful to see how they apply to a movie that had immediate commercial success matched by lasting critical approval. Made in 1938, Jean Renoir's *Grand Illusion* served as a bridge between productions of his such as *The Crime of M. Lange* and *The Marseillaise,* on the one hand, and *The Rules of the Game,* on the other.

The former were part of his politically engaged and somewhat optimistic search for human solidarity, while the latter reveals his greater pessimism as Europe prepared for war.

If we study formal techniques that Renoir deploys to good advantage in *Grand Illusion,* we can see, for instance, how artfully the camera moves back and forth in discussions between the French officer (played by Pierre Fresnay) and the German commandant who imprisons him (Erich von Stroheim), and how this technique expresses Renoir's ideas about the ambivalent relationship between these two men. When Jean Gabin, as another French prisoner, has been thrown into solitary confinement and is befriended by a guard who acts kindly toward him, the camera prepares us for this by panning through his cell in arc-like movements that simulate a comforting embrace and therefore present another gamut of human possibilities. Formalists might argue that these and related uses of the camera constitute a cinematic discourse, with a "syntax" of its own, that enables Renoir to communicate as he does throughout the movie.[5]

If, however, we wish to interpret the same film as an example of Renoir's devotion to realism, we can stress equally well his accuracy in portraying the life of combatants in World War I, their experience as prisoners or as captors, the class system that controlled wartime mentality as pervasively as it did when Europe was at peace, and so on—all this rendered by photographic images that resemble the physical appearances of persons and places vividly portrayed through realistic icons of actualities within the narrative. In the last scene, when the French escapees reach snow-covered terrain and are not fired upon because the Germans assume they must be in Switzerland, the realism of both the setting and the situation indicates, as Stanley Cavell points out, that this film "is about borders" as they exist in human nature.[6]

In view of what the formalist and realist interpretations succeed in doing, they are each a valid methodology. But they can also be seen as cooperative rather than competitive. *Grand Illusion* is not only about borders. It is also about efforts that people make to overcome whatever separateness causes war or dissension. It reflects our desire to achieve oneness with other human beings regardless of their nationality or station in society, and thus to attain friendship or love of different types. In its ontology neither this nor any other film can *duplicate* social, material, or spiritual realities. The originals can be represented, but only through transformations that adapt them to the needs and circumstance of cinematic art. However great its likeness to some object, no image can have the kind of being that this actuality retains as just the unique and transient entity that it is. Film reproduces reality by recreating it, by transforming it through the visual and auditory technologies designed for that purpose.

To say this, however, is to say that realist and formalist approaches are both required, whether to understand the nature of film or to analyze valued instances of it. In films we view the world and its reality, but only through transformations that could not occur without the formalist techniques a filmmaker introduces to convey the thoughts, the feelings, and the overall attitudes expressed in his or her conception.

By examining the technical details of a film we learn how its transformations are produced, and how they affect the audiences they can reach. The images made and organized by the camera are of little interest in themselves or in their formal structure. What strikes the eye must also reach the mind and heart. Whatever its theme or subject matter may be, a film has meaning only because it is about the world as observed from a viable perspective. While recognizing this, a clarified realism supplements that much of formalism that is also defensible.

As with all meaningful communications, there are in film various levels of transformation. Having agreed that *Grand Illusion* is not a replication of anything, we may then perceive that its transformations of physical appearances directly influence the way it transforms the realities of human separation and oneness to which I referred. This can lead us to consider how cinematic transformations deal with questions that philosophers ask about the meaning of separation, oneness, autonomy, or social and interpersonal life. Such investigations may also be treated as transformations, in their case ideational, that do not re-present reality but rather revise and reanimate it through philosophical imagination. In experiencing a film, we immerse ourselves in the complexity of all these transformations as they interact cinematically. What we identify as the movie we are watching is an embodiment of the meanings-for-us that eventuate.

I

1

Appearance and Reality

We often recognize the difference between how things seem to be and how they really are. The fact that a straight stick looks bent when it stands in water has intrigued even the most primitive observers. One can easily be deceived by similar perceptions that recur throughout our experience. For a philosopher like Plato they are not quirks within the physical world but rather clues to our condition as human beings. The example of the stick in water implicates our visual sense itself, Plato claims, and indirectly every sensory capacity that we normally have. And if our vision can be illusory, should we not say the same about all other types of sensation? Is not experience as a whole liable to distortion and inaccuracy at any moment? Obviously it is, and therefore Plato and his successors believe that only through acts of reason can we penetrate beyond the deceptiveness of ordinary life. Such philosophers think our rational faculty is able to reveal the ultimate truth about empirical events. Through it, they maintain, we can make contact with reality, which presumably belongs to a realm of

being that is distinct from the world of appearance proffered by sensation.

As in its many variations throughout the centuries,
Plato's line of thought is one that only a philosopher
would pursue. It tries to explain not specific occurrences
or moments of consciousness but rather all of them in
life. Reality is envisaged as transcending whatever appears in our experience, which is therefore metaphysically inferior or deficient to that extent. Apart from its
rational component, human existence is considered just
a passing image of what really is: our senses are not only
fallacious about that underlying reality but also sullied
by their own inherent imperfections. From this, Plato
and those who follow his lead infer that there must be
some moral and even aesthetic flaw in the world as we
ordinarily know it. That world is inextricably dependent
on sensory awareness. It is a realm of appearance in
contrast to reality.

More than any other philosophical doctrine, this belief in an ultimate dichotomy between appearance and
reality pervades most of our conventional ideas about
good and bad, right and wrong, true and false. It issues
into the split between nature and spirit that I sought to
overcome in my book about their possible harmony.[1] The
split is present in all traditional thinking in the Western
world about the nature of art.

I return to this distinction now because of its direct
but elusive relevance to theorization about film as well
as other visual and dramatic media. Explicitly in the
representational arts, and implicitly in those that are
nonrepresentational, each medium deals with reality in

ways that are characteristic of itself. Watching a stage performance, for instance, we see real human beings who portray fictional characters although their presence as living men and women in a theater partly determines our aesthetic response. The actors are there as persons who look the same as people we might meet outside, but the characters they enact inhabit whatever region of imagination the drama presents to us. That is why we call the actors "*performers.*" We do so in a way that is comparable to our saying that farmers perform a useful service when they plant their crops. The reality of a farmer consists in being a person who uses imagination for the sake of growing foodstuffs. The actor employs imagination in the making of fictional impersonations. It is a different activity and a different type of imagination. But as someone on stage whom we take to be performing in his or her profession, the actor is real to us as both a human being and a participant in a productive enterprise—just like the farmer, though their roles are not the same.

I emphasize these two kinds of reality in the aesthetic experience of a play in order to understand what happens when people and situations that exist in the ordinary world are summoned up and put to creative service in this art form. The characters are born in the playwright's mind but made available to the audience by actors performing in collaboration with the director, the stage manager, and others involved in each production. Reality is represented and expressed through their cooperative presentation of the fiction. The viewers see an integrated whole that is both real and imaginary.

In the context of these preliminary remarks, the following question now arises: What, in this kind of transaction, can be deemed appearance and not reality? In Plato's view, all of it. That is why he spurns art as being just an image of an image. He holds that the people on stage are only temporal instantiations of ultimate and eternal forms of being. And since these instances of humanity function as conveyors of possibilities proffered by the playwright, the artwork in which they perform must be an image of some other image. Plato believes that art is by its very nature primarily appearance, and different from science or (rationalistic) philosophy inasmuch as these attempt to get beyond appearance instead of enlarging it through imaginative make-believe. Science and philosophy penetrate into the structure of reality, Plato thought, and do not fabricate a substitution for it.

In a sense Plato is surely right. Art is thoroughly artificial in a way that science and philosophy are not. These disciplines try to discover the objective truth about our being, or at least about specific aspects of it. Art takes a different approach. Its use of imagination is more radical. Art is free to invent fictional entities in fictional settings that have no direct correspondence to existence. In nonrepresentational media art may regale us with sights and sounds that have never been seen or heard before. Though it can provide its own type of truthfulness, art does that by altering our acquaintance with reality instead of investigating it systematically.

These alterations occur in particular operations of imagination to which I will presently return. They are all designed to produce an artifact that is consummatory in its totality, unlike the products of science or philosophy. Those justify themselves by their fidelity to factual observations and our sense of how things really are. Though scientists or philosophers may feel happy if they think they have discovered "the truth," the methods and the findings of their investigations frequently conduce to no one's happiness. But art is not like that: it employs the freedom of its artificiality to construct something that will be enjoyable for its recipients in view of what matters to them.

An account of this sort would not be acceptable to Plato. He would note that it obviates any need to make a metaphysical distinction between appearance and reality. Plato himself recognized that this basic tenet is not verifiable. In Book VII of *The Republic* he nevertheless offers the Myth of the Cave as a parable Socrates invents to recommend his distinction between the two realms of being. Whether or not the doctrine is defensible in itself, Plato's myth has been interpreted by some scholars as a forerunner of twentieth-century theories about the nature of film.

Socrates asks us to imagine a group of people who have been imprisoned and chained in a cave since early childhood. They sit and stare at a wall on which shadows are projected by their guards, whom they never see. What the prisoners do see are reflections of objects that the guards move around without letting the prisoners have any knowledge of what is happening. Being unaware of anything else, the prisoners take the reflections to be real objects in the world. Once they have become habituated to the shadowy figures before them, they cannot think of them as only images. If someone were to tell these people that, outside the cave, things in the sunlight exist as the originals for what appears on their wall, they would assume this person is crazy. Whatever they see is for them reality.

Though Socrates' myth may be sophistical insofar as it predicates what must be proven—namely, that there is an objective realm unknown to us because we are imprisoned in experience that contains only appearances—his account might be true as a myth about art in general. Some philosophers have defined the aesthetic attitude as absorption in whatever the artist presents as real although it is just an imitation of reality. While patterned pigments on a canvas are real as what they are, we experience them as a part of representational painting only if they stand for something that has its being in the outer world. In that sense the presentations in this medium may be said to be "reflections" of reality. But since we can respond to these reflections as we do to real objects, is there not an element of deception in aesthetic experience? Various philosophers have thought there is, and therefore they consider art an "illusion" comparable to what Socrates portrays as the condition of the prisoners in the cave.

As against this interpretation of art, we may argue that the aesthetic attitude need not be, and normally is not, illusory. That is the position I will be defending. But what if there were an art form explicitly developed to create images of reality that can mesmerize the audience so completely that it treats these presentations as if they were the realities they depict? Would the spectators not be living in a state of appearance much as Plato's prisoners do? And would they not be like the spectators who become enthralled by the shadowy pictures projected on a movie screen? Even if Plato's distinction between appearance and reality is unacceptable as metaphysics, it might possibly serve as a model for understanding the art of film.

Theorists who have been excited by this possibility belong to either of the two schools I mentioned in the introduction. One emphasizes the fact that the photographic image, whether in moving or still pictures, seems to duplicate real objects even if it cannot do so literally. All realist theory is based on this crucial claim. The formalist approach is attuned to the manner in which even a realistic presentation, however absorbing it can be, is very different from anything in the real world that may have been photographed. Compared with what we usually perceive in life, cinematic images are tremendously distorted, expanded in some respects and truncated in others. If we nevertheless respond to them as the realities they resemble, must this not be due to subjective reactions that each filmmaker artfully instills in the audience? Most formalists in film theory are committed to this view.

Formalist thinking about appearance and reality in relation to film issues from philosophical idealism of the nineteenth century. To my knowledge, no one has fully examined this derivation. I will not be making that attempt in this essay, but I see the linkage in the work of the German-American psychologist Hugo Münsterberg. His book *The Photoplay: A Psychological Study*, originally published in 1916, is an early but major effort that is now being read anew.[2] In opposition to the common belief that art, and especially film, is an imitation of nature, Münsterberg emphasized the degree to which all artistic presentations include unrealistic effects. The uniqueness and aesthetic promise of film he ascribed to the medium's exemplarly power to reconstruct the real by imagining it not as it is in itself but as it would be if it conformed to the faculties of the human mind. That approach was characteristic of idealist philosophy, and it underlies formalist film theory in its entirety.

Münsterberg notes that the focusing of attention, which occurs in ordinary consciousness, has heightened importance in all aesthetic experience. Watching a stage production, however, we may have difficulty trying to focus attention as we should. We are easily distracted by the fact that the actors are men and women whose individual attributes exceed whatever the playwright wants us to see. A meaningful glance, pivotal at some moment in the drama, may go unnoticed by people in the audience. In film the problem is handled by a close-up that forces us to attend to what the filmmaker had in mind. Eisenstein and many other formalists would later argue, in a similar fashion, that *only* film can have the requisite ability to communicate meanings through purely visual effects.

Münsterberg suggests that the reliance on attention as a mental phenomenon is just one of the many ways film transmutes reality into a simulacrum that conforms to subjective structures of human consciousness. He makes parallel remarks about the experience of depth, movement, memory, imagination, and emotionality. Though the cinematic image is two-dimensional and nothing moves on the screen that presents it to us, we see the content of the film as three-dimensional and in motion. Instead of resorting to an uncertain memory of what happened earlier in the story, as would be the case in a stage play, film can use a flashback to show us what we are supposed to remember. Though imagination permeates all of human experience, and excels in every art form, film gives imagination control over space, time, and causality to a degree that is unequaled by any other visual medium.

Münsterberg also remarks that the directness and vivacity of film can have an enormous impact upon an audience's affective response. Cinematic experience causes identification with the feelings of characters in the drama, although (or possibly because) there is no living person being responded to. Movies evoke emotional reactions that may sometimes be stronger and deeper than any we permit ourselves in the real world.

Later theorists have carried this line of analysis further than Münsterberg. But I find his ideas particularly interesting because they illustrate how film theory can be influenced, to its detriment as I will argue, by idealistic philosophy as well as by the traditional distinction between appearance and reality. Objective idealists believe that our experience of the world *determines* the character of reality. While Münsterberg does not explicitly make this ontological claim, he interprets film as an art that successfully molds reality to the qualities of the human mind. Having maintained that the close-up "objectifie[s] in our world of perception our mental act of attention" and that in film generically "it is as if reality has lost its own continuous connection and become shaped by the demands of our soul,"[3] Münsterberg defines the nature of cinematic art in terms of the following "unified principle":

The photoplay tells us the human story by overcoming the forms of the outer world, namely, space, time, and causality, and by adjusting the events to the forms of the inner world, namely, attention, memory, imagination, and emotion. . . . The massive outer world has lost its weight, it has been freed from space, time, and causality, and it has been clothed in the forms of our own consciousness. The mind has triumphed over matter and the pictures roll on with the ease of musical tones.[4]

There is much that is quite plausible in this conception. Through contrivances such as zooming, panning, flashback, flashforward, and all the rest, the filmmaker can put images on the screen that violate the spatial, temporal, and causal coordinates of the world we consider real regardless of our involvement with it. These images have their aesthetic effectiveness because they contribute to psychological processes that alter the audience's conscious response. Extending Münsterberg's approach, recent psychologists have explored the role played by operations of the mind they deem "unconscious" in one sense or another. Properly understood, these too can help explain the phenomenology of film. Nevertheless the overall view is suspect as a general theory.

For one thing, it imposes an erroneous conception of film psychology. According to Münsterberg, spectators of a realistic movie recognize that the events being dramatized in the narrative represent possible occurrences in the world, and yet, he claims, the presentation of these possibilities is *felt* to be unreal or fictional since it results from the mental constructs definitive of cinematic art. Though we know the movie is about "objective reality," Münsterberg insists that the film situation causes us to experience something else, what he calls "a product of our mind."[5] But this idea falsifies the actual state of affairs. The audience involved in watching a film replete with close-ups or flashbacks, or whatever, pays no attention to the fact that the images being seen are unlike the outside world.

On the contrary, as spectators we accept film techniques as instrumentalities that give us access to some imagined reality. We do not think that the images *conform* to anyone's mentality, either our own or the filmmaker's. Though independent reality is not present in a film, it is represented by the transformations that enable us to make sense of the images that are present and *resemble* the real world. Reacting to these images, through our intellect and through our feelings, we respond to some prior reality as it has been transformed by techniques characteristic of this medium.

Münsterberg is misleading when he states that in film we never experience the real but only the outcome of its having been molded or re-formed by agencies of the mind. It is true that without these agencies film could not portray the world as it does. What we see, however, and what we feel, is meaningful to us because of realities that we are familiar with in life. Even if we keep reminding ourselves of specialized knowledge we may have about the nature of film—for instance, that it is based on directorial decisions and the vicissitudes of performance before the camera, whose images then appear as two-dimensional pulsations on a flat surface—our experience of a movie transcends this information about modes of presentation.

Münsterberg's film ontology illustrates how greatly the Platonic distinction between appearance and reality exerts a controlling influence. Through its dependence upon processes of the mind, film is interpreted as an advanced development in the realm of appearance. As a result, reality itself can be reached only through investigations that do not adapt the real world to the mental one but rather, as in science or philosophy, subordinate the mental world to the real one.

All the same, Münsterberg does not think that film is inferior to either science or philosophy. He describes aesthetic experience in terms that underline the importance of art while setting it apart from any search for knowledge about the world. He sees art as an attempt to liberate things or events from their usual entrapment in nature, thereby separating them from the rest of our existence and allowing us to delight in their mere appearance. "The work of art," he states, "shows us the things and events perfectly complete in themselves, freed from all connections which lead beyond their own limits, that is, in perfect isolation."[6] This being what he takes to be the function of art in general, Münsterberg then applauds the "superb enjoyment" that film provides in its special ability to bring about its own kind of perfect isolation.

Throughout this book I will be arguing against all attempts, in either the ontology or aesthetics of film, to distinguish between appearance and reality. Such distinctions presuppose that consciousness or experience can have a being that is totally different from the more ultimate being designated as uniquely real. The view assumes the perspective of some ideal spectator observing at a distance events, things, or persons that exist in a self-enclosed and somehow unreal domain separate from the reality of either this observer or the world as it is in itself. The sense organs of the audience are consequently thought to display visual, auditory, and other data that may indeed originate from what is real but never present it as it really is. Taken as the manifestation of detached mentality, photographic images are considered appearances that occlude reality whether or not they look like it.

Art cannot remedy the situation these philosophers depict, but its capacity to make appearance delightful and arresting encourages a thinker like Münsterberg (different from Plato in this respect) to idealize the aesthetic attitude. Münsterberg defends the art of film by suggesting, in effect, that it is a technologically superior means of coping with the insurmountable split between appearance and reality.

But are we willing to credit any systematic belief in that split? In a movie theater, as in other aesthetic circumstances, the audience does observe something more than, and different from, external reality. But that is because the *meaning* of what is seen is not itself on the screen. Nor is it in the mentality of the spectators. It issues from a transaction, as real as any other natural occurrence, between the objects or events being portrayed, the images that resemble them, and the responsive men and women in the audience who have learned how to experience the medium of film. The flickering photographic images are realities in themselves, but their capacity to transform other kinds of reality gives them their place as an intermediary between the audience and the world that is being represented. The meaning of the transformations that infuse cinematic art cannot be limited to any one of these elements.

Nor can they be compartmentalized as Plato and Münsterberg believe. A scientist or philosopher does well to remind us that much of what we ordinarily consider real may not be the same as things as they are in themselves. It is nevertheless counterproductive to assert that the world we do experience, or any depiction of it, is just an appearance whose isolation from what is real and ultimate can be an aesthetic virtue. The aesthetic is not a separation from reality, but rather a consummatory trope by which we give meaning to our immersion *in* reality.

The meaning that film art proffers is a function of the specialized techniques it has devised. Münsterberg's analyses of these techniques, as well as their psychological effects on the audience, are often useful and revealing. They help explain how films differ from staged productions or even other forms of visual art. But none of this justifies the conclusions that Münsterberg draws.

In characterizing techniques in film as contrivances for making reality conform to processes of our mind, Münsterberg misrepresents the function of these techniques. The close-up does provide a means of focusing attention upon something the audience might otherwise fail to notice. But it does not introduce another kind of object; it does not substitute a mental being that negates the individual reality to which it addresses itself. On the contrary, the increased attentiveness, like all the other film effects Münsterberg studies, enables the filmmaker and the audience to communicate with each other through discovered and created meanings they both care about. This is similar to what happens in the everyday world apart from film, or any other art. Without these interactions the world would make no sense to us, and we would not make sense to ourselves—we would not be human beings or the different persons that our systems of value-laden meaning turn us into.

Far from changing reality into aspects of a separate mind, cinematic techniques are creative in another manner. They transform perceptual experiences we have already had by placing them within a different context of meaning. The new meanings that arise out of cinema exist only in relation to its audience. This development of cognitive and affective life is neither mental nor physical, neither subjective nor objective. It is a construction of meaningfulness that defies the polarizations implied by any dualism we may have inherited.

If we make that shift in our thinking about film ontology, our conception of the medium will be significantly different from the one that is presupposed by Münsterberg or the later formalists. Nor will our standard of film excellence be the same as Münsterberg's. He asserts that film aspires to the condition of abstract music. As music is free to express feelings and ideas through tones alone—through sounds in their auditory purity, liberated from any need to depict or represent reality—so too, he says, is film ideally suited to the presentation of visual images joined in a kind of symphonic unity and fashioned by the mental processes that are peculiarly cinematic. Münsterberg's doubts about the aesthetic utility of synchronized talk, as in talking motion pictures, is related to this belief about the value of unadorned, and hence unfettered, visualization.

I will return to the dichotomy between cinematic sound and sight in the conclusion of this book. But as a contrast to the idealism built into Münsterberg's formalist approach, I must first consider the realist philosophy that has also played a role in film theory. As always, my goal is the harmonization of both alternatives.

Toward that end it will be helpful to examine an article by one of the few great philosophers who have said anything interesting about the nature of photography. In a lecture given more than eighty-five years ago entitled

"The Photograph and the Mental Image," George Santayana, at that time a younger colleague of Münsterberg, outlined an ontological approach that foreshadows much of what the realists would later say. Though Santayana refers only to still photography, his comments can stand as a point of departure for understanding the realist conception of film. If only because Santayana's words have had so few readers, they are worth quoting at length as a philosophical prolegomenon to further discussion of the realist position:

... while photography is surely an art and its products are often beautiful, there remains a deep and quite unbridgeable chasm between it and that other kind of art whose essence is not so much to mirror or reproduce the outer aspects of things, however bewitching, as to create in imitation of the processes of Nature, but in different materials, things analogous to the natural. These products of creative art are shadows rather than replicas of reality and present things as they could never have actually existed: men of stone, passions that obey the rules of prosody, heart-throbs that keep time with an orchestra, tragedies that unravel themselves in five acts without irrelevant incidents—in a word, substitutes for reality that transform it into the materially impossible, in order to bring it within the sphere of the persuasive and the divine.

Now a photograph is produced by a machine, just as the images of fancy and memory are reproduced by a machine; both the camera and the brain transform their impressions in many ways, but not as a moral and conscious interest would transform them. The accidental transformations of the image in photography and memory are consequently defects and imperfections, while the intentional transformations of ideal art are beauties. For the function of photographs and of mental images is to revive experience, but the function of creative art is to interpret experience. Creative art must transform the object, in order to tell us something more about it . . . There is one art to focus and revive experience, there is another art to digest and absorb it. The one is an artificial memory, the other a petrified intelligence.[7]

I have chosen this passage from Santayana because it incorporates various concepts that have been held by theorists of film as well as still photography. The statement has a coherent unity that is both suggestive and far-reaching. Nevertheless the major theses seem to me suspect, and the general argument erroneous. Santayana's view is as follows: (1) There exists a "quite unbridgeable chasm" between photography and the more traditional arts, this chasm resulting from photography's essence as that which mirrors, reproduces, duplicates, revives, and in general records reality. (2) Photography manifests its being as a duplicating art by reproducing "the outer aspects of things," the physical dimensions of reality as they show themselves in some visual appearance. (3) Since photography is an art that focuses and revives our experiences, it relies on visual percepts emerging from memory rather than the extravisual concepts of an intelligence that digests and absorbs. (4) Photography does not interpret experience or intentionally transform its object, since it operates by means of the automatic technology of the camera as a duplicating mechanism. In this chapter I discuss the first of these tenets, returning to the last three in subsequent chapters.

Writing when he did, it is predictable that Santayana would not have mentioned motion pictures. But as we know, many writers—Bazin and Kracauer, for instance —have argued that "ultimately" or "basically" cinema is a photographic endeavor that duplicates and records reality in a manner that pertains to photography as a whole. In "The Ontology of the Photographic Image," Bazin describes film as an improvement within photography's reproductive mission that confers upon the movies "a quality of credibility absent from all other picture-making. [Through film] we are forced to accept as real the existence of the object reproduced, actually *re*-presented, set before us, that is to say, in time and space."[8] Kracauer, too, maintains that "the basic properties [of film] are identical with the properties of photography. Film, in other words, is uniquely equipped to record and reveal physical reality and, hence, gravitates toward it."[9]

Bazin and Kracauer recognize that film does more than just record, and Kracauer later goes on to distinguish between the recording and the revealing properties of film. They would agree with Santayana, however, in thinking that film and still photography differ from all other arts in having as their final nature the reproduction and recording of reality. It is here that we encounter a major difficulty in their approach. In what sense is the photographic image, whether in still or moving pictures, either a *reproduction* or *recording* of reality? The picture looks just like the object, one might say. This is surely true in some respects, even though picture and object are very different in many others—in depth, luminosity of color, palpability, etc. For the moment we can ignore these differences. That will help us concentrate on the fact that looking *like* something, even looking *very much* like something, is not enough to say that a reproduction or recording has occurred. There are physical relations that enter in.

Not only does the photographic image resemble its object, but it is also the result of a causal process involving that object. To state that the camera reproduces reality is, in part, to assume the prior existence of something in the world that has been linked within a chain of events that includes the camera's chemical and mechanical attributes. If we know the properties of both the object and this mediating mechanism of the camera, we can reliably infer what the photographic images will look like. Nothing comparable can be said about arts such as painting or sculpture. But Santayana and the realists in film theory assert more than that alone.

Saying that the photographic image reproduces reality without interpreting or intentionally transforming it, Santayana, at least, has in mind the notion of ontological identity that his mature philosophy elaborates in his doctrine of essences. The photograph is thought to reproduce reality by capturing its essence, or more precisely, those essences that are co-present in some visual appearance, or, even more precisely, I would think, a subset of them as selected by the camera. Whatever the refinements to which this conception would have to be subjected, it predicates that in looking at the content of a photographic image we see it as having the same being as some object in the world that has been photographed by the camera. The photograph reproduces reality in the sense of duplicating the object's being, which is then present in the image as a further instantiation of the essences the two have in common. Since photography consists in the mere replication of essences, an unbridgeable chasm separates it from arts that revise and re-create what is given in reality.

Though Bazin and Kracauer may have known nothing about Santayana's ideas about the realm of essence, this interpretation of his argument is faithful to what they say about photographic realism. Santayana speaks for them when he calls the photographic image a "literal repetition." In my opinion that is where all three make their fundamental mistake. I find their view wholly unconvincing, primarily because it is so foreign to any experience I myself have had. I have never perceived a literal repetition in the relationship between the content of a photographic image and the object that has been photographed. Moreover, I believe this to be true of everyone else. In observing photographic images, we normally experience them *as* photographic images, which is to say that their content seems quite distinct from any object in the world.

In processing our perception, whether arresting a single moment of it or yielding a succession of them that registers on our sensorium as the seeing of continuous motion, photography imposes a spatial frame that eliminates peripheral vision. It thereby transforms the object, if only by the way we see its portrayal. We have a dynamic interaction with objects that we perceive in nature, and this disappears once a photographic image makes its presentation of them. However similar the reproduction may be, the object is not literally repeatable in this different kind of experience. Aside from trompe-l'oeil photography, we are always aware—even in our moments of cinematic absorption—not only that the image is different from a percept but also that its content is a transformation of perceived realities. The world can be represented, and in a sense reproduced, by photographic images, but it cannot be re-presented or duplicated as the realists claim.

Far from lending itself to literal duplication by photography, reality becomes photographically imagized by the camera. Our realization of this underlies the wonder that we all feel in the presence of realistic photography. What looks so much alike is nevertheless so *different* —not just different in some of its details, but also onto-logically different. To say that the photographic image reproduces reality must therefore mean something unre-lated to a literal repetition.

In answer to my criticism, the realists might reply that photography differs all the same from arts that make no attempt to *record* reality. But even here their outlook, which now turns on the concept of recording, seems untenable to me. I see no reason to think that essentially, by its fundamental nature, photography is geared to the recording of reality. That implies that the photographic image must be used to preserve and retain (or, as Santayana puts it, "revive") something in the world that we wish to experience secondhand. An "artificial memory" provides this service. But there is nothing in photography that *requires* it to function in that way, and as an art form it often operates in totally different ways.

Thinking of photographs as recordings, Santayana would seem to be referring to snapshots taken as reminders or else as visual accounts. Even at the turn of the century, however, there existed a large class of still photographs that aspired to artistic and even literary goals that have little to do with either preserving reality or reviving it.[10] And the same has been true of motion pictures almost from the beginning of their existence. With the exception of home movies, or those that photograph special occurrences for historical or scientific purposes, films are not usually made as recordings. The realists are confused about this because they fail to recognize that a recording is a *particular,* not invariable, use to which the photographic image may be put.

For example, consider the Russian documentary *Victory Parade in Moscow's Red Square.* This film, made immediately after the end of World War II, is primarily a record of the triumphant parade that took place in Red Square. The camera sits in the reviewing stands as an impassive spectator of what occurs in front of it. The film lasts almost as long as the parade, or at least its principal segments. The documentary was made for distribution throughout the Soviet Union so that the many millions of people who could not come to Moscow or fit into Red Square would be able to see what they might have seen if each of them had actually been sitting in that part of the stands. More recently, we often find similar uses of the camera on television, but I prefer this example because it is so thoroughly simplified, depending as it does on what seems to have been a single stationary camera. It is therefore a clear case of how film can be employed for the purpose of recording.

Without trying to show us many aspects of reality, *Victory Parade in Moscow's Red Square* presents only the ones that its audience is likely to find interesting. Similarly, the recording of a symphony orchestra will be limited to sounds that music lovers prize. Nor does it reveal what the conductor or any of the performers hear. Though resembling whatever appears on the record, the music they experience is not relevant in this context. As a recording, the final product, like the film I have mentioned, is designed to reproduce elements of some prior reality that are being preserved for subsequent repetition.

My argument against those who identify the ontology of film with recordings of visual reality is briefly this: Most films are not recordings, and so the realists have failed, at least to that degree, in their analysis of the photographic image. While every identifiable image can possibly serve as a recording, and, compared with mirror images or memory images, the photographic image is extremely adept at this because of its permanence and forceful impact, only occasionally and with special intent do filmmakers make recordings of any sort. Familiar as we are with the type of documentary that I cited above, we recognize it as an idiosyncratic and hardly representative use of the motion picture camera. What narrative films, and many other documentaries, do is not at all the same.

The point I am making does not turn only on the fact that cameras are selective in how they process the world. In that regard verisimilitude recordings are similar to fictional transformations. Imagine people in a field trying to record the sound of a robin. They will arrange their sound equipment in the hope of eliminating unwanted noises, and they may explicitly concentrate upon one or another quality of the robin's song that they consider worth preserving. To the extent that they succeed in faithfully reproducing this actuality, we may readily accept the outcome as an authentic recording. But regardless of what the individual product may be, whether as an auditory datum or as a visual trace, all recordings are surrogates for something that existed in the world and was located in a space and time related to the operation of the recording apparatus. Our attention must be directed to the external object not only as an entity that resembles what we are allowed to hear or see but also as a prior being that is the causal basis of our interest in the eventual reproduction.

To understand what recordings are, we must have some knowledge of the human circumstance in which the mechanical process has been deployed. That gives the outcome meaning. Furthermore, the concept of recording implies that this transformation is subservient to its original, encouraging our imagination to go *through* the created image or sound for the sake of attaining some chosen reality that preceded it in nature.

At the same time, almost every recording asserts its own dignity as against its mere condition as an instrumentality. Listening to the recording of a symphony orchestra, we generally hear it as *music*. Though we know the sounds are a replication, we attend to them as if they were being played afresh for us in our living room. There is no incompatibility between something being heard or seen for the sake of what it records while also being experienced in itself as a new presentation. And by a queer twist in logic, perhaps it was this that caused so many theorists to assume that all films must be recordings, even though relatively few of them are.

Thus I find it hard to believe that recording and reviving reality is the primary goal of photography. Even the most realistic shots in a movie are rarely recordings of anything. On location in a modern city, the camera will scan across the physical appearance of buildings, bridges, streets that do indeed exist, that we may recognize, and that possibly look to us more or less the way they did when we were there ourselves. Their presence in the film may have a significant effect upon the dramaturgy. But the lifelike images are not recordings. They exist as landmarks to a creative imagination beyond themselves.

Far from recording anything, these artifacts ordinarily belong to what I have elsewhere called "the imaginary." I will analyze that concept more fully in chapter 3. The appearance of real objects has obviously been copied, and fidelity to the original may even be of great importance (depending on the work of art—in Olivier's *Henry V* cardboard cutouts were most effective for some of the distance shots, but in Antonioni's

L'Avventura they would have been ruinous). Whatever the value of realistic shots, however, they are part of the fiction, if the film is a fiction, or the supervening message or historical report if it is not. Treating them as recordings would deflect our attention away from the artistic function these photographic images were made to have.

Even if film and still photography were often used as recording devices, it would be hard to see why this should create an unbridgeable chasm between them and the more traditional arts. If we think of how many paintings have been devoted to the reproducing of visual appearances in the hope of making a permanent record—portraits, views, celebratory scenes, events that were sometimes imaginary, sometimes real, sometimes uncertain in their classification—we must conclude that the recording capacity of photographic imagery is by no means a property it alone possesses. We might say that the invention of photography brought with it the ability to make *better* recordings, and in some regards this is certainly true. The machine reproduces tiny details in a way that human beings can barely approximate. The camera is exceptionally adept at making recordings. That need not be doubted. What I am denying is the idea that its recording capability makes photography essentially (rather than technologically) different from the older art forms.

These other visual arts are like photography inasmuch as they also provide recordings on many occasions; and it is like them to the extent that its nondocumentary uses involve an elimination or submergence of its recording aptitude. Above all in narrative films, the realistic images exist for the sake of aesthetic effects that are comparable to those in the more traditional arts. If there are chasms, they are not unbridgeable.

To some people it may seem like philosophical quibbling for me to deny that the photographic image is basically, inherently, a recording, particularly since I admit that this is one of the functions to which the camera lends itself. But I have labored the point because there is a great deal at stake. In asserting that film is by its nature a recording, theorists like Bazin and Kracauer claim to have found a definition that reveals the fundamental ontology of the medium. Although Bazin is a wonderfully open and receptive writer, he clearly thinks that seeing film as photography and treating photography as a "transference of reality from the thing to its reproduction" enables us to determine not only what film is but also what it can do.[11] By contesting this kind of theory and its underlying beliefs about appearance and reality in film, I am questioning the doctrine's suppositions about what is truly cinematic.[12]

If I am right in saying that photography is not *essentially* a recording device, we cannot characterize the aesthetic quality of its medium as a literal "repetition" or "re-presenting" or "capturing" of reality. And if we choose to use such language metaphorically, we will have to refine it more than the realists do. We will have to study the many other ways in which photographs and films can be works of art, whether or not they meet the standards imposed by the dogmas of realism.

In taking the path I am recommending, we may wonder whether the ontology of the medium can tell us much that helps solve the problems of aesthetics. Whether or not a photographic image contributes to artistic excellence, it belongs to a class of entities that we readily distinguish from the physical properties that exist in spatial matter. Like a mirage in the desert, the photographic image is not palpable. (The screen can be touched but not the image that is projected upon it.) It resembles a mirror image in providing a bidimensional likeness of a real object. It is similar to a retinal image in being a result of visual processing. In other ways it can be likened to a memory image, an eidetic image, and various types of mental images. We know what it is for something to be an image, though a precise definition may be difficult to formulate. In saying that the photographic image is a member of that class, are we saying very much that is revelatory about the nature of art?

Possibly not. Ontology may have only limited importance in relation to film theory or the evaluation of cinematic artworks. Nor should we expect our philosophical analyses to answer all of the interesting questions about the *camera obscura*, the mechanical and chemical forces upon which photography depends, the dynamics of projection upon a screen, and so forth. Technical decisions about angles of the lens, placement of the cinematographic instruments, cutting, editing, choice of coloration—all this goes beyond ontology. Whatever lens the cameraman selects, the photographic image will have the same category of being. In itself, ontological insight is neither aesthetic nor nonaesthetic. It offers its perspective to each alike, and therefore it alone cannot tell us how a medium like photography may culminate in great artistic creations.

At the same time, faulty ontology about the relationship between appearance and reality can distort one's panoramic conception of this art. As philosophers of film, we should always be aware of that danger. It is not, however, unavoidable. Having clarified our ideas about the nature of the photographic image, we may possibly find that we have transcended much that is troublesome in realist as well as formalist aesthetics.

These reflections lead me to some of the problems in Stanley Cavell's attempt to continue the tradition that Bazin and Kracauer represent. In order to show how film is rooted in reality, Bazin spoke of the photographic image as a kind of "fingerprint," a "tracing," an "impression" of the object, a "mold in light," and even a "casting" (as of a death mask). Cavell is dissatisfied with the notion of photographs being molds or impressions or imprints because these "have clear procedures for getting rid of their originals, whereas in a photograph, the original is still as present as it ever was."[13] Cavell means that, in manufacturing images of the world, photography maintains the "presentness" of the world itself. Though the world is not present on the screen in the same way in which it was initially present to the camera, Cavell claims that it is equally present, as present in its filmic projection as it was when the camera took a picture of it.

In saying this, Cavell uses the words related to "presence" as terminology that is relevant to the ontological issues he discusses. I cannot pretend to perfect clarity about the configurations of this concept, which emerges from a long history in philosophy and theology, but I presume that its contours overlap significantly with ideas about focus of attention, awareness, precise apprehension of what is given to us in sensory experience, and in general an intuition of consciousness as it moves through space and time.

Assuming that this interpretation is correct, it seems to me that, in the sense Cavell intends, the world is *not* present to us in the photographic image. What is present is only the photographic image itself. It has been created to resemble the world in certain respects, and unless these resemblances were evident to us, it would have none of the meaning that it does have.

One could even say that what is present to us in the photographic image are the resemblances themselves. They are not illusions, since the nature of cinema prevents us from confusing the image with things in the real world. In fact the presentness of the photographic image is forced upon us by our knowledge of conditions that explicitly *preclude* our confusing the image with any prior reality: the flatness and two-dimensionality of the surface, the enormous size to which the objects have been magnified, the artificiality of the shimmering light in the darkened hall. The aesthetic import that photographic, in this case cinematic, images attain results from the vividness with which they present themselves under these circumstances. The sheer immediacy of the images contributes to the powerful impact that film can readily achieve. But it is not the presentness of the world that operates in this manner.

As for that much of the world that has been photographed, its aesthetic relevance must always depend upon its recognized absence from the images that provide so many engaging likenesses to it. Cavell says that "photography maintains the presentness of the world by accepting our absence from it."[14] But in the photographic experience we are not absent, as Cavell seems to think, from the world as a whole, though we are of course absent from the persons or events that have been photographed. Images are also part of the world and they are very much present to us. It is because they are *constantly* present, with all the liveliness that cinema can muster, that we are able to experience vicariously those absent realities that have been transformed into artistic elements.

Believing that the photographic image shares the being of the model it reproduces, Bazin argued that a film screen is not a frame, as in a painting, but rather a mask that cuts off the rest of reality. Similarly, Cavell states that photographs are of the world as a whole since, unlike paintings, they are continuous with the reality that goes beyond their borders. This suggests, however, that the world of a painting exists completely within its frame, so that we cannot ask what lies beyond, whereas the content of photographs or films is presumably the real world itself, as it extends outside in all directions regardless of how much of it has been cropped for the purpose of photographic art.

Here again one feels that aesthetic discrimination has been hindered by faulty ontology. For it is only a special kind of photograph that implicates the reality of objects beyond its borders, as it is only a special kind of painting that fully contains itself within the frame. It would be quite appropriate to assume that to the right or left of what appears in a painting by Guardi or Canaletto there existed other buildings and canals in eighteenth-century Venice. Such paintings rely upon this type of inference, exactly and as much as a photographic rendering of the same scene does.

On the other hand, it would be bizarre for us to look at a Hollywood movie about a town in the old west and to infer that in one direction there really were ranch houses of the nineteenth century, in the other an actual saloon, up the hill a graveyard populated by people who lived and died in that period, and so on. If we are not shown these bits of reality, we give no thought to them, and they are not part of our aesthetic suppositions. Though the photographic image will show us what the sets look like, as mediated by the camera used in the shooting of the film, we know they only represent a town that could have existed a hundred twenty years ago. We would not assume that the town itself exists beyond the frame. We might not see the sets as the hollow and insubstantial constructions that they are, but neither do we take the cinematic images as anything more than a portrayal of some town that *may* have once existed. If, in the absorption of the film experience, we respond to the presented image as if we were looking at a real street with a western town all around it, this is because we have been captivated by the sheer presentness of the image itself. Our response is an act of imagination, not a literal perception of the reality being displayed.[15]

More recently than Cavell, Kendall Walton has sought to renew the realist position by arguing that the pictures yielded by photography are "transparent." According to him, the camera is a "prosthetic device" on a par with the telescope or microscope and therefore different from the implements used in even realistic paintings. Being inherently prosthetic, Walton claims, film presents reality in a way that is analogous to the presentation afforded by telescopes and microscopes (or for that matter, opera glasses or ordinary eyeglasses). As we say that these help us to see the real object, and not just its image or representation, so too, Walton insists, we should say that it is the object itself we see in photography.

What Walton ignores, however, is the fact that prosthetic devices such as those he mentions are instruments for *augmenting* our visual capacities. They allow us to see things that are distant, small, scarcely perceptible, or even invisible to the naked eye. These are things that exist in a space-time continuum coherent, often co-present, with the body of someone who uses the relevant artifacts. In the film experience the situation is not like that. Even when it makes a recording, the camera is not prosthetic in the sense of extending our visual acuity. It merely gives us access to what *it* can see. The camera belongs to the spatial and temporal continuity needed for its realistic operation, but we do not.

Though we have a direct bodily connection to the images that the camera enables a projecting mechanism to flash before us, we have no such tie to the objects that have been photographed. In films that are not recordings, there might not even be isomorphic objects, regardless of how realistic the images may be. To this extent, film—and photography in general—is neither more nor less prosthetic than painting. In their transformation and reconstitution of the world, filmmakers resemble El Greco when he rearranged the position of buildings in his painting of Toledo. Though they may not alter the visual pattern as much as he did, the filmmakers change our experience of it through the meanings and techniques their art form employs.[16]

In the realist ideology there resides a belief that reality can be captured and made present on film much as a wild beast can be captured and then presented to the public in a zoo. But this analogy does not hold. All that can happen in the film experience is that the public may be captivated, as I have said, and this signifies something very different. Whether or not a film is a recording, there is nothing in its ontology that can present us with the real world outside. Reality can be represented, possibly duplicated in the sense that a transformed version of it is made, but in itself it cannot be caught and put on display. A work of art, be it a painting or a photographic film, is "realistic" insofar as the images are faithful in their likeness to pertinent aspects of an external object. But only the images are presently real to us, even though they are real as a semblance of what is not now present.

An effort that has artistic merit is one that captures
our attention and willingness to enjoy what is being
offered us. It snares our receptivity to itself as a source
of consummatory experience. It does this by guiding our
imagination through aesthetic channels that lead us to
accept both realistic and nonrealistic effects as appropriate for its overall design. In the process we may also find
that even the most artificial effects reveal realities whose
meaning would have escaped us apart from our aesthetic involvement. The meaning we thus acquire may
affect us as true about the world, and we may feel that
we are in touch with its reality as never before. Superla-
tive works of art do present us with the absent world
—but only in the sense that it has been given meaning
through insightful representations of it.

The job for filmmakers, as for critics, theorists, and
philosophers, is to discover how a cinematic artist can
activate the requisite imagination of just those people
with whom he or she wants to communicate. The communication itself occurs through a transformation of
reality that defeats any doctrinaire distinction between
appearance and reality.

I can make this point more concretely by analyzing a
Woody Allen film that places the question of appearance
and reality at the core of its narrative. When his movie
was released in 1985, Allen called it the best work he had
done. It can have considerable utility for our discussion.

In the magical ecstasy of the moment of descent, Tom steps out of the screen looking even larger than he did as an image on it. The close-up that presents this accentuated magnification makes the character seem like a looming monstrosity in a horror film.

2

The Purple Rose of Cairo

Avoiding the usual distinction between appearance and reality as well any fixed dichotomy between formalist and realist modes of thinking, we now may find ourselves better equipped to harmonize what is best in the alternative theories. The ideas I have suggested thus far, and will continue to develop throughout this book, are mainly concerned with problems in the philosophy of film. But they also have ramifications for film criticism and the analysis of individual movies. Treating cinematic efforts as transformations of reality, as consummatory means of communicating with other people, as the outcome of an imaginative quest for meaning and for truth through techniques available to filmmaking, will help us experience films without preconceptions about the medium as either a recording of reality or else as an imposition of formal or merely technological manipulation.

Woody Allen's film *The Purple Rose of Cairo* finds its inspiration in the issues we have been discussing. As Allen says in a newspaper interview, he wanted this movie to be an "entertaining" presentation of "the difference between fantasy and reality and how seductive fantasy is and how, unfortunately, we must live with reality, and how painful that can be."[1] This may serve as an adequate account of the initial stimulus that might motivate an artist, the bright idea that gets him started. It reveals the nature of Allen's intention, although it scarcely indicates the character of his achievement. But what is it, we may still ask, for something to be a "fantasy"? And what is it about "reality" that makes its painfulness aesthetically interesting?

One might say that the film answers these questions through its narrative about Tom Baxter, the handsome and charming character in a popular movie, who descends from the screen and woos a spectator (Cecilia). When she agrees to run off with the actor who created this character, and above all when she has to return to her unhappy marriage, she may be seen as one who "lives with reality" and finds "how painful that can be." Yet this, too, tells us hardly anything about Allen's film. Even its title reverberates aesthetically throughout our experience of the work. An essential element, an important personage, so to speak, within the movie is another movie also entitled *The Purple Rose of Cairo*. That film, henceforth in my text specified by italics in quotation marks, is a thirties Hollywood escapist comedy-romance designed to raise the spirits of people in the Depression who could use it as a commodity for vicariously enjoying the life of carefree opulence they imagined to be a reality for the happy few with plenty of money and savoir faire.

The film within the film is in black and white, very effective for accentuating the blackness of the tuxedos and the whiteness of the formal shirts and gowns. Its style and coloration contrast it with the drab but authentic coloring of the theater in which the movie is being shown as well as the coffee shop where Cecilia works, the apartment she lives in, and the town in which it is located. Her New Jersey town is close to, but infinitely removed from, the "madcap Manhattan adventure" of the escapist movie, and incalculably distant from the Egyptian pyramid in which some of its characters first meet each other.

To call "*The Purple Rose of Cairo*" a fantasy is more or less correct. Though it does not portray events that run counter to our knowledge about nature and its laws, it leads people like Cecilia to avoid the truth about their marital and economic woes. Movies of its sort have become addictive for Cecilia. She turns to them whenever she feels defeated by the hardships of everyday life, and in their constant enjoyability she finds an indiscriminate anodyne that nullifies the possibility of any lasting change in her condition. The fantasy world she inhabits is not, however, illusory. When she enters the theater, she knows that she will be seeing a make-believe, a product of the filmmaker's imagination, just as we also know that Allen's film depicts events that never happened and some that are incredible.

His work is therefore a fantasy in a different sense. It not only requires us to suspend disbelief but also to penetrate beyond that suspension for the sake of experiencing realities that can be comprehended only through an extraordinary, a literally extra-ordinary, flight of artistic imagination.

What is the nature of such imagination in this case? We are alerted to its special character by the fact that we observe a movie *about* a movie, not just a movie that includes a movie within it. There are many films of the latter type: for instance, *Whatever Happened to Baby Jane?*, or *Sunset Boulevard*, or more extensively *Day for Night*. Those films have moviemaking as part of their plot, and in varying degrees they deal with the actual process of film production. But they are not about the nature of movies. In *The Purple Rose of Cairo*, on the other hand, the ontology of cinema functions as an important part of its content. To that extent the film is about itself *as* a film. It illuminates what all films are—at least, all narrative films.

Some philosophers have claimed that artifacts become aesthetic objects when they are self-referential in the sense that they tell us about the nature of the medium in which they occur. That would have to be argued separately. We would need to know whether this requirement can be shown to apply to all works of art. And what would count as the "telling" that is presumably essential? Without engaging this particular problem, it seems clear to me that fictional constructions that focus upon the ontology of their own medium, whether as film or as anything else, attain a gamut of metaphoric and aesthetic significance unique unto themselves. The metaphors can be of different kinds. In *The Purple Rose of Cairo* they are mythic and religious.

That becomes evident when we consider the opening and the closing moments of this film. It begins with Fred Astaire singing voice-over (from the movie *Top Hat*) the song by Irving Berlin that includes the lines: "Heaven, I'm in heaven / And my heart beats so that I can hardly speak. / And I seem to find the happiness I seek / When we're out together dancing cheek to cheek." The entire movie revolves about this metaphor of heaven. The song's first reference to it even coincides with the logo of the distributor (Orion), which shows a cluster of stars circling rhythmically in the black sky. The film ends with Cecilia watching the scene in *Top Hat* in which Astaire sings the song and then dances with Ginger Rogers to the music of it.

During the dance sequence Rogers leaps and twirls in an exuberant and triumphant culmination that counterpoints Cecilia's defeated mood when she first entered the theater. She has learned that Gil Shepherd, the actor who portrayed Tom Baxter, has deserted her. She is unemployed and knows she must now return to the miserable life with Monk, her apelike husband. Yet as she watches the jubilant dancing of Astaire and Rogers, she is enthralled by the spectacle, engulfed in their movie as she has been in so many others before.

The lighting on Cecilia's face then brightens ever so slightly, her eyes glisten, and a tiny smile of joy and resignation appears as the camera makes its terminal fade-out. She is not in heaven; she is not out dancing with anyone; she is sitting alone once more, unlike the other people in the theater who are there as couples; she is unaccompanied by the husband who considers movies "junk"; and yet the screen conveys to her some image of a heavenly domain. Romantic movies like *Top Hat* and *"The Purple Rose of Cairo"* are, for her, epiphanies of a better world than the one she is trying to escape. Her glimmer of a smile suggests that she may well have benefited from her painful history. It gives her access to a reality greater than anything else she finds in life.

Within this mythological frame, the thematic fantasy of Allen's movie can be taken to be Cecilia's mystical experience. As in more traditional narratives about mystics, she is a person of little importance to or for the world: she seems incapable of succeeding in ways that others value, and in fact she is socially impaired and a failure in her marriage. Even the prostitutes whom Tom encounters seem happier and more secure than Cecilia. They know how to make a buck, as one of them suggests, whereas she cannot hold down a job even with her sister's help. In the innocence of her ineptitude, Cecilia has a vision of grandeur that transcends this world. She converses with a being of superhuman origin, an imaginary creature who performs a miracle in descending from the screen and behaving like a real, but also ideal, person.

In the magical ecstasy of the moment of descent, Tom steps out of the screen looking even larger than he did as an image on it. The close-up that presents this accentuated magnification makes the character seem like a looming monstrosity in a horror film. We think of mythological accounts of females raped by gods and sometimes driven mad or even incinerated by relations with an overpowering divinity. People in the theater scream and a woman faints. Stunned though she is at being singled out as worthy of such attention, Cecilia remains receptive. When the supernatural entity talks to her and takes her hand, she submissively runs off with him. She is obviously at home within her vision.

Thinking of Tom as a monster in a horror film may also elucidate why that genre has been exploited so successfully by moviemakers. Whether the monster is an enormous gorilla living on a tropical island, or an off-shoot of nineteenth-century European technology, or an up-to-date mad but brilliant American scientist like Hannibal the Cannibal, he represents an alien reality that may well fascinate a susceptible female. Confronting this creature from that other realm of being, the audience is compelled to visualize the threat it poses as well as the even more frightening possibility that the monster may somehow be superior to ordinary human beings. Worse yet, we may find ourselves feeling love or sympathetic identification toward the monster. Horror films reverberate within these affective dimensions.[2]

Though Cecilia is at home in her contemplation of Tom, he is not at home anywhere. He leaves "*The Purple Rose of Cairo*" because he wants to be what he calls "real," which is to say, like Cecilia. Meeting Gil, who claims to have "made him live," he is told that he can never be real. When Tom insists that it is something he will learn, Gil ridicules that as impossible: "You can't learn to be real. It's like learning to be a midget. It's not a thing you can learn. Some of us are real, some are not."[3]

We laugh because of the absurdity built into the notion of "some of us." Who are the "us"? Fictional beings as well as those that are not fictional? It is the common verbiage used by bigots who feel prejudice toward other people, or other forms of life, on the basis of some ad hoc criterion of difference, however arbitrary it may be. Are the real ones among us only those who have come into existence the way that usual men and women do? Gil might seem to be an authority about reality, since he is a successful actor on his way to stardom and therefore cognizant of how one survives in what we call the real world. But much of the humor in this scene turns upon the fact that we have just observed a radical emendation in what everyone accepts as reality and the laws of nature. If Tom can walk off the screen as we have seen him do, why should he not be able to learn how to be real? It may be hard, we say with a chuckle, but anything is possible now.

Or, at least, it would be if we retained our faith in the mythological fantasy. But the point about this movie is that Cecilia does not, and since it is she who creates the parameters of her own mystical experience, the level and quality of her faith control what will or will not be its eventuality. Her decision about its denouement occurs when she must make her choice between Tom and Gil. Both insist that they love her—quite a reversal of fortune since heretofore no one has. In deliberating, she says of Tom: "I just met a wonderful new man. He's fictional, but you can't have everything" (434). On the other hand, Gil is what he himself calls "an actual human." In opting for Gil, she tells Tom: "See, I'm a real person. No matter how . . . how tempted I am, I have to choose the real world" (459).

As Sam Girgus remarks in his analysis of this movie, Cecilia's reasoning is ironic since what she chooses as the real world is "Hollywood, the epitome of the unreal."[4]

In that glamorous but deceptive place to which Gil is luring her, she would find nothing to equal the reality of what she has been experiencing with Tom. When Gil deceives her in true Hollywood fashion, she finally realizes her mistake. She learns something about the ambiguous duplicity of the real world that her innocence had kept hidden from her before. But now it is too late for her to join Tom. He has gone back to the screen, and *"The Purple Rose of Cairo"* has not only been shut down but also burned in all its copies.

As a result, Tom is eternally homeless, existing neither as a fiction nor as an actuality. Cecilia survives but only as a kind of widow in the reality of daily life. Though she will probably remain in her marriage to Monk, her love for Tom will be an insuperable barrier between them. Tom will linger in her memory of him, like the long since dead teenager Michael Fury in James Joyce's *The Dead*. And as Greta in that story, and in John Huston's film version of it, invokes the spirit of her departed friend after hearing a tenor sing the Irish ballad that Michael used to sing to her, so too does Cecilia experience an epiphany of her love by attending the Astaire/Rogers movie whose song we heard at the beginning. Though Tom has been destroyed even as a fiction, he belongs to the heavenly reality of film art that recreates itself whenever Cecilia renews her mystical devotion.

The mythic burden of her quest for reality can also be revealed by noting that Tom and Gil, both played by one actor, have the same physical appearance, as if they were a single person divided within himself. That is the premise exploited in world myths about "the double": man and his shadow, the body and the soul, humanity belonging to nature as well as spirit. Film is itself an analogue of this theme, its mobile images being awesome doubles for the objects they represent.

In the legend of Amphitryon, whether in Plautus, Molière, Kleist, or twentieth-century adapters like S. N. Behrman, Jupiter descends as the double of a human being whose wife cannot distinguish him from her husband. When she learns the truth, she opts for the person who belongs to her reality and rejects Jupiter's offer to make her immortal as he is. The experience becomes shattering for the woman but it ends in her giving birth to a higher type of life, partly mortal, partly divine, which is Hercules the savior of his people.

Cecilia's mystical fantasy leads to something that is metaphorically similar. Having transformed her existence by bestowing upon it a meaning it could not have had before, her afflatus manifests the spirituality of art that enlivens human nature and is present even in escapist movies.

Nevertheless, we may ask, what might have happened if Cecilia had had sufficient faith to give herself completely to the kingdom of heaven she believes in? She takes a tour of it, like Dante in his trip to paradise, when Tom pulls her through the screen and into *"The Purple Rose of Cairo."* But, like Dante, she knows quite well that she does not belong among the celestial host. Buster Keaton's dream sequence in *Sherlock Jr.* enables him to participate in the narrative of the movie he had been watching, but Cecilia has no role to play in the cinematic reality Tom inhabits. In fact, her presence there is so disconcerting that the show cannot go on. Meeting her, the chanteuse at the Copacabana passes out as if Cecilia were to her what ghosts or ghoulish visitors from "the other world" are to us. Delightful as Tom's fictional life might seem when they spend their madcap night on the town, Cecilia realizes that it can never be her own.

But since *The Purple Rose of Cairo* is make-believe, it could have finished with Tom and Cecilia walking off together toward some imaginary sunset in the real world, comparable to the closing shot of *Modern Times.* That film also portrays the harsh conditions many poor people were enduring throughout the Depression, and it, too, shows that art—singing and dancing in the restaurant—can offer a possible escape. When the tramp and his young friend are banished from even that hope of social redemption, they walk into nature, on a country road, leaving civilization behind. We do not know where they will go, but we have digested the message of the film, which is that modern times are not worth living in.

This may seem more pessimistic than Allen's movie, and yet Chaplin's ending has an uplifting effect. The man and the girl, both vibrant in their creative ingenuity, have each other. The romantic dream lives on in their isolation from the rest of reality. They smile as they march hand in hand toward the distant hills. It is dawn: for them the sunset is a sunrise.

The Purple Rose of Cairo lacks this assurance. Tom having been annihilated, we cannot believe that any other romantic character will ever step off the screen and into Cecilia's arms. She is doomed to the limbo of knowing what heaven is but also remembering that she could not remain in it as she may have wanted, either by marrying a Hollywood actor or by uniting with his personage within a movie. Allen is forced into this conclusion by his staunch rejection of any benign or sentimental resolution. The real world being what it is, he refuses to shield us from the fact that Raoul Hirsch, the producer of *"The Purple Rose of Cairo,"* his publicists, his lawyers, and the business world they represent must demolish the monstrous being they—like Frankenstein or many other perpetrators of horror—have unknowingly brought to life. However "perfect" Tom may be, he is just too dangerous as a legal hazard. The nature of his perfection is something of which they are not even aware.

One might say that Cecilia recognizes that Tom is perfect because she is in love with him. That is built into the romantic philosophy that the film both questions and reembellishes. But Cecilia is also in love with the movies from which Tom emanates. The Hollywood mogul and his entourage are not. They are engaged in making money and advancing their careers. Even Gil is surprised when Cecilia says that Tom is perfect. Before the scene in which he informs Tom that he can never be an actual human, Gil tells his agent that he had "worked so hard to make him real," to which the agent replies: "Yeah, well, maybe you overdid it" (382). Obviously, real for Gil means being like himself. Tom is something else. What he is, exactly, concerns the Hollywood people not at all. It never occurs to them that Tom's phenomenal feat might have some intrinsic value, might reveal truths about humanity that science has not yet uncovered, or might even be an opportunity for them to make more money and further their careers in new directions.

Responding to Tom as she does, only Cecilia can appreciate his ideality. The fantasy she experiences in her attempt to overcome her sense of worthlessness presents him as a Christ figure who arrives on earth in order to offer a lowly person like herself love and understanding absent in the life she has had thus far. His being an image of Christ may also explain why he must die or be extinguished, and why this world has no place for him. As the respectable inhabitants of Gadarene say in Richard Wilbur's poem about Christ's reception when he comes to their community: "If you cannot cure us without destroying our swine, / We had rather you shoved off."[5]

Dostoyevsky's Grand Inquisitor expresses the same type of sentiment, though not as crudely. The Grand Inquisitor believes in the divinity of Christ but wants him to stay in his heavenly abode and not interfere with the church's administration of the world he sought to redeem. That separation between the two realms reinstates the distinction between appearance and reality that mystics like Cecilia repudiate in their sense of oneness. Though she cannot return Tom's love (when he offers her perfect sex, she is unable to respond to it, saying only "I'm not that kind of girl"), Cecilia becomes an object of idealization herself.

This appears most exquisitely in the scene in the brothel. Tom goes there because Emma, one of the prostitutes, whom he instinctively knows to be a kind-hearted person, invites him to see where she works. Being perfectly pure, he has no awareness of what prostitution is. When he learns that it involves making love, having sex, with a person that one does not love, he gently explains to the fetching women that he has no desire for sexual dalliance since he loves only Cecilia: "I'm hopelessly head over heels in love with Cecilia. She is all I want. My devotion is to her, my loyalties . . . Every breath she takes makes my heart dance." Not knowing who or what he is, Emma can only reply with that mixture of idealistic longing and realistic disbelief which resonates through all of Allen's films: "Are there any other guys like you out there?" (429).

Emma's question is richly suggestive, since it voices an undying hope for perfect love that even someone who trades in imitations of the real thing may harbor still. Cecilia has been singled out as the unique object of such love; at least, she is the only one in this film who receives it. Telling Tom what the world is like, she mentions that people get old and sick and never experience "true love." He answers that things are different where he comes from. Cecilia remarks that in real life you don't find the right kind of person. Tom replies: "You have" (379). And indeed her moments with him reveal that when appearance and reality mingle, rather than being kept in separate realms of ontology, there may occur a consummate love that issues from this unification. Such love, as idealists in the nineteenth century might have said, may well be the meaning of life, and thus show forth the nature of reality as well as appearance.

In being a perfect man/god who sanctifies the life of ordinary mortals through his spiritual presence, Tom is supremely real in his fictional state—which is to say, in his appearance as a personage in a romance film. His brief excursion into the outer world discloses not only the untenability of distinguishing between appearance and reality in the manner of traditional theorization but also the possibility that what appears in works of art can be more real than events in the world we usually consider real. This philosophical tour de force is intimated in a brief exchange between two other participants in *"The Purple Rose of Cairo."* Henry, who has the role of a "sophisticated playboy/writer," suggests that the characters define themselves as real and the audience in the theater as "illusion and shadow . . . You see, we're reality, they're a dream." The tough old countess in his movie sneers at this proposal: "You've been up on the screen flickering too long" (437–438).

Ten years earlier Allen had toyed with similar issues in a short story entitled "The Kugelmass Episode." Trying to flee his loveless marriage, a professor of humanities in New York enlists the aid of a magician who transports him into the world of *Madame Bovary.* It is surely not coincidental that the prostitute in *The Purple Rose of Cairo* has the same first name as the protagonist in Flaubert's novel. Kugelmass experiences ecstatic sexuality in the arms of Emma Bovary and feels as if he is really living for the first time in his life. His troubles begin when she wants to savor the delights of Manhattan and pursue a stage career on Broadway.[6]

Despite its clever choice of Flaubert's fiction, which aspires to the condition of simple realism, "The Kugelmass Episode" is little more than an anecdote humorously presented. To see how Allen's film could have germinated out of it, we should turn to Luigi Pirandello's *Six Characters in Search of an Author*. However indirectly, it is a source that provides the basis for Allen's inventiveness in *The Purple Rose of Cairo*.

In his play, Pirandello regales us with three dramas simultaneously. There is the realistic account of the stage manager and his company of actors rehearsing in their theater; there is the confused history of the six characters acting like real people and searching for the author who conceived them but never wrote out their saga; and finally there is the inclusive attempt by the characters to use the stage manager, and then the actors, as the means by which they can realize themselves as living, though partial, beings. The play we in the audience finally observe in an actual theater, or read at home, is the third of these. It is the drama we think of as Pirandello's completed play. It derives from the interaction between the two other dramas.

Something similar is true of Allen's film, except that "*The Purple Rose of Cairo*" is already finished, indeed shown to us on the screen, and the characters in it deal with the calamity that Tom's absence causes by leaving their habitual roles and behaving like actors who have only been impersonating characters. This affords comedic effects not present in Pirandello, but the fundamental structure remains the same. Pirandello described his work as "theatre in the theatre"; Allen could have called his "film in the cinema."

In Pirandello's play the characters chaotically and piecemeal recount their family tragedy. It is a story about the all-enduring Mother who has borne children by two men, about the Father who may or may not have thrown her into the arms of her lover, about the Step-Daughter who has had sex with the Father in a house of assignation, and about the Son who repudiates but cannot evade their mutual sorrow. Only the Father and the Step-Daughter seek a rationale in all this. They believe that in making the family members live as characters the unknown author had an inner meaning for each of them.

In view of this belief, the Father claims that they are more real than the actors who will portray them if the stage manager agrees to take the place of the author and present their story. The Father argues his case as follows:

Ours is an immutable reality which will make you shudder when you approach us if you are really conscious of the fact that your reality is a mere transitory and fleeting illusion, taking this form today and that tomorrow, according to the conditions, according to your will, your sentiments, which in turn are controlled by an intellect that shows them to you today in one manner and tomorrow . . . who knows?[7]

Reasoning this way, the Father would seem to be offering a justification for Henry's suggestion in *The Purple Rose of Cairo* that the word *real* be redefined to refer to the characters in the movie rather than the audience watching it. In fact, one might remark that what the Father says applies to film even more than to the theater. The appearance of characters on stage varies from production to production and from performance to performance, depending on successive changes in the directors' conception, the actors' interpretation, and even the audiences' responsiveness. But characters in a film are fixed securely in the photographic imagery that illuminates them. Apart from physical deterioration of the celluloid, they remain invariable in their recurring presentations. Their being emerges from the perennial repetitiveness of mechanized matter. They do not react to any audience, and though they, too, depend on a director's conception and an actor's interpretation of their personality, this happens only once. The characters come into life not through a succession of performances but in the single act of making the movie. That is what fleshes them out, to use an expression that Gil employs twice. Until it happens, even the screenwriter is only a preprogenitor.

The wittiness of Allen's fantasy is augmented by the fact that we see the characters of "*The Purple Rose of Cairo*" confronting their calamity with all the unpredictability of people who exist in time and space. Having been imaginary toads in real gardens, which was Marianne Moore's definition of art, they have now become real toads in an imaginary garden. Though Tom is the only member of the cast who leaves the screen, the others respond to this event in ways that do not belong to their script. As a consequence, they all forgo the kind of reality that Henry wished to assign to them and that the Father in Pirandello considers greater than the reality that real men or women have. If we laugh, it is because our habitual assumptions about appearance and reality have been overturned so imaginatively. Moreover, we recognize the bitter wisdom, typical of Allen's view of the human predicament, in the press agent's commentary on this situation: "The real ones want their lives fiction, and the fictional ones want their lives real" (395).

We earthy characters in the real world have often yearned to share the blissful condition of those who are purely fictive. When she enters into the black and white movie, that happens to Cecilia. She is shocked to discover that what passes for champagne there is really ginger ale, but she obviously relishes hopping from nightclub to nightclub with the rapid abandon conveyed by the Hollywood dissolves of neon-lighted marquees parodistically blending into one another while different types of music suggest the popular dances that joyful clients are performing in each hot spot. By changing the fictional scenario, however, she and Tom destroy the static constancy of film reality. Free to do whatever he wishes, Arturo the waiter now delights the Copacabana's patrons with a tap dance, which he could never have done before. One can only wonder how the other characters use their newfound state of being.

In this glorious merging of appearance and reality, we are afforded the spectacle of enhanced possibilities that include the freedom real people have as well as the completeness within preestablished limits that constitute the nature of fiction. That consummation defines what Sartre calls the for-itself-in-itself, the ontological perfection that consciousness craves but that nothing in existence can attain. According to Sartre, this imagined ideality is the harmony of facticity and transcendence that God has necessarily and would have in actuality if only he existed. As aesthetic surrogates for any such divinity, Tom and the other personages are enclosed in a paradox beyond their control. If they are characters in a film, they must be the same from performance to performance. If they are free to change, as real people do, they can no longer serve as merely the products of imagination. They cannot be both, and that is their tragedy.

Sartre would say that human beings also seek a reality of both sorts: we unceasingly want to attain God's perfect being—we want to *be* God, Sartre claims—even though the nature of existence defeats our aspiration. That is the human tragedy. But from this it would follow that the argument of Henry and the Father cannot hold. Despite the programmatic fixity of the characters, they are no more real than the audience that thinks of them as just appearances. However much the characters may embody possibilities the audience longs for but can never realize, they do so only as emanations of a reality they do not have apart from the being of people who live in nature with all the volatility and incompleteness that life entails.

On the other hand, the audiences at a film or theatrical production discover in these representations of themselves a meaning in their own reality. Through the unreal artificiality of art they can sometimes learn what they really are. They might not have acquired this self-knowledge in any other way.[8]

In *The Purple Rose of Cairo*, Tom tries persistently to find out what he is. At first he explains his defection from the screen by saying that he wants "to live." Ontogeny recapitulating phylogeny, he begins his exploration into the nature of his being by experiencing the adolescent feeling that just to *live,* with freedom and chromatic intensity, is all one needs for a good life. After Cecilia takes him to a church, he reflects with greater maturity about the meaning of existence. When she says that God is Tom's creator, he identifies him with Irving Sachs and R. H. Levine, the authors of his script, whose Jewish names seem comically appropriate in view of Allen's religious origins.

Cecilia quickly corrects Tom's misconception, explaining that God is bigger than the two writers or even the production in which they were involved. She tells him God provides a "reason for everything" and without him life would be "like a movie with no point, and no happy ending" (408). In his search for meaning, Tom then ponders, as he later informs the women in the brothel, about God "and his relation with Irving Sachs and R. H. Levine"—which is to say, Woody Allen (424). We are told nothing further about Tom's theological inquiry.

In the preface to his play that Pirandello wrote after it had become a classic and therefore subject to multiple misconceptions, he defends the Father's ideas. He states that, unlike lovers in the real world, whose passionate attachment wavers and often disappears as the months or years go by, the oneness that unites Paolo and Francesca in Dante's *Commedia* is forever the same each time we open that book and read about it. Hearing Francesca's recital, Dante faints away, which signifies to me that in his great commiseration he cannot accept the idea that a deity who is omnibenevolent would allow the lovers to be punished as they are. But Pirandello suggests a different interpretation. He says that Dante's swoon reveals his attunement to the "living and sudden passion" that eternally reanimates Francesca's words every time they are uttered, in however many readings. Pirandello explains this by remarking: "All that lives, by the fact of living, has a form, and by the same token must die—except the work of art which lives forever in so far as it is form."[9]

In this reification of artistic form, Pirandello would seem to be clinging to the dualism, primordial in the Western world, between appearance and reality. Though Pirandello's view is not strictly coherent with Plato's, since he gives the aesthetic an ontological dignity that Plato officially denies it, he nevertheless reflects the thinking of Neoplatonists such as Plotinus and those theorists in the 1920s who were influenced by him. Plotinus thought it was through art, and not through a necessary transcendence of it, that we can reach the ultimate reality of the Platonic forms.

And yet, what Pirandello shows us in his play, as Allen also does in his film, is something that Plato and Plotinus would each have rejected. In neither the play nor the movie, nor the movie in the movie, is the author present. We know the names of the screenwriters of "*The Purple Rose of Cairo*," and Raoul Hirsch, the producer, converses with the distraught characters after Tom has left the screen. We surmise, and Pirandello's preface confirms, that Pirandello himself is the author who had the idea of the six characters and then abandoned them.

But we never see the characters in either play or film being created and we have no access to any intelligence that would justify the notion that they instantiate an abstract form or essence.

With the same repetitiveness that occurs in all our readings of Francesca's speech, we do see a couple of scenes from *"The Purple Rose of Cairo"* occurring time and again in perfect duplication of themselves. Yet their *meaning* is never given to us as a separate reality, and even if we knew what was intended by the creators of either the film or the play, or of Dante's *Commedia*, we could not conclude that this intentionality defines the form, let alone the "eternal" form, that reveals the characters' unique and possibly superior reality. That would have to show itself in the meaning each work has within itself, and not in an author's prior intention.

The reality the characters do have depends on the aesthetic transformations created by the photographic images, or theatrical enactments, or in the case of Paolo and Francesca the literary effects, that each artist fabricates for the delectation of the audience, whose members must individually make sense of what appears in a relevant experience of the work being presented to them. In principle, at least, the same thing happens throughout human existence, whether or not one is involved in an aesthetic transaction. Neither the artist, nor anyone else, has a metaphysical pipeline to eternal forms.

In the recent analysis of Allen's film to which I referred earlier in this chapter, it is called an expression of "post-structuralist anxiety." The movie's treatment of the relationship between appearance and reality is thought to illustrate the now familiar belief that no approach to works of art can justify itself as a revelation of meaning that exists apart from some audience's interpretation of them as aesthetic constructs.[10] This notion is, however, too extreme. It errs in denying that an author's intentions, about which he himself may be quite knowledgeable, can sometimes have legitimate importance in what counts as a reliable understanding of the characters he has created. That clue, or even insight into what they are and represent, does not disclose an *authoritative* meaning, as if they issued from a realm of being that only the artist can identify. His or her intentions are never definitive in any essentialistic way, and we cannot hope to use them as an objective standard for adjudicating what the characters "really" mean. But neither can we infer that an author's intentions, assuming we know what they are, must always be irrelevant.

Correspondingly, we should not think that every audience has equal access to the meaning of an artwork. We can only say that as our experience of the actual world is more than just a hodgepodge of appearances, as opposed to some higher reality that only a philosopher can reach, so too are works of art—and above all, the fictional characters in them—neither illusory images of the world they portray nor perfected realities unencumbered by mutabilities that might relegate their audience to a lower level of ontology. Artistic productions, whatever their meaning may be and whoever is fully qualified to understand it, are appearances that have their own reality as creations that can sometimes express truths beyond science or philosophy. Art does not separate appearance and reality. Nor has it reason to.

By playing imaginatively with stock ideas about appearance and reality, and by inventing a fable in which they blend or overlap, *The Purple Rose of Cairo* questions our naive acceptance of these ideas. It shows us that in all of life, whether in art or in the psychological and economic conditions that we may try to circumvent through our immersion in the aesthetic, appearance and reality are always interwoven with each other. Plato's metaphysics is thus discarded, and in that sense disproved.

Though films are not alone in this achievement, they have a quasi-miraculous aura that can possibly make them more amenable to it than any other medium. In painting or still photography, reality is presented in a frozen mode. That is their wonderment, as Keats recognizes in his "Ode on a Grecian Urn." In literature and in music, our experience of reality is mediated by written or sonic abstractions. In the theater, we see live human beings but in settings that are blatantly unreal. Only in film, only in the mesmerizing dance of its stroboscopic effect, is the liveliness of apparent reality so greatly enhanced as to beguile us with the feeling that what we are observing is real enough to warrant its captivating our attention.

That, of course, is the idea that underlies all realist film theories. But through its fanciful mythology, and through the brilliance of its artificial absurdities, a film like *The Purple Rose of Cairo* supports the formalist approach as well as the realist.

To explain the appearance of reality, which is identical with the reality of appearance, we require both methodologies. Allen's film is a masterful comedy that helps us envisage, and enjoy, the possibility of their harmonization. It transcends the suffering in life by transforming it through aesthetic imagination. Like all great art, it thereby sustains and fortifies the human spirit, as even philosophy may do occasionally.

II

3

The Visual and the Literary

For those who think of cinematographic art as inherently a mechanical recording of the visual world, it is natural to believe that this art must adhere to the "outer aspect of things," the surface manifestation of material reality. Erwin Panofsky makes this assumption central to the argument in his celebrated essay on "Style and Medium in the Motion Pictures." All the earlier representational arts derive from an "idealistic" approach, according to Panofsky. He says they start with an idea that the artist projects upon shapeless matter rather than originating with objects that belong to nature itself. Only film uses physical entities as the basis of its artistic effort: "the movies organize material things and persons, not a neutral medium, into a composition that receives its style, and may even become fantastic or pretervoluntarily symbolic, not so much by an interpretation in the artist's mind as by the actual manipulation of physical objects and recording machinery. The medium of the movies is physical reality as such . . ."[1]

Kracauer and some of his realist followers make similar remarks. For instance, Michael Roemer, in an article suitably entitled "The Surfaces of Reality," argues that "the camera photographs the skin; it cannot function like an x-ray machine and show us what is underneath. . . . The medium must render all meaning in physical terms. This affinity for real surfaces, combined with great freedom of movement, both in time and space, brings film closer than any other medium to our own random experience of life."[2] In the writings of theorists like Zavattini in the early 1950s, one can see how ideas such as these served as a justification for the neorealist movies of various filmmakers in Italy and elsewhere.

As a mere philosopher, I have no desire to deprive artists of any perspective they find beneficial to their creativity. But I do feel the need to point out that a decision to eliminate flimsy plots and implausible fictions does not have to be defended by claiming that the photographic medium presupposes a special and peculiar fidelity to physical reality. An artist who wishes to do so may take the "outer aspect" of things as his subject matter. If he does, he will find that cinematographic art—like all the other visual arts—is well disposed to this aesthetic interest. With the camera in hand, the filmmaker can reproduce appearances and play across their surfaces. He may explore and investigate their unique effects, possibly expressing, if he is a great artist rather than a mere technician, important truths about the human experience of them.

To say that film has a special linkage to real surfaces is, however, either trivial or misleading: trivial if one only wishes to remind people that the photographic image is the image of something in the world that has been photographed rather than x-rayed; and misleading if one then concludes that the reality of life that an artist seeks to display, to interpret, and to clarify can be revealed through nothing but the portrayal of physical surfaces. In a film all meaning must indeed be *established* in physical terms, since photography presents us with images, which are physical entities. But the meaning of these images belongs to more than just the surface appearances themselves. That is what the realist theory fails to recognize sufficiently.

Some writers seem to believe that films gravitate toward the surface of physical reality in the manner I have been questioning because they think the seeing of a cinematic image is identical, or very similar, to our ordinary perception of things in the world. But there is now ample evidence to indicate that the two types of experience are distinct from one another. The film image resembles the retinal image, which is quite different from an actual percept. Perceptual images of sight result from the brain's processing whatever retinal images have been transmitted to it. In perceiving the world, we have a retinal image of something that might be called surface reality, plus brain action upon that retinal image. When we see the photographic image, however, we have a retinal image *not of the world* but of the camera's quasi-retinal image plus brain action on our image of the camera's image. To this extent alone, film experience involves transformations of what appears as physical reality regardless of how realistic the filmmaker may wish to be, or how much he or she cares to use the camera as a recording device.

One might even say that it is because the cinematic image is different from the ordinary perceptual image that neorealist filmmakers have been able to go beyond Lumière and others who sought to do little more than duplicate surface reality. Zavattini speaks for Rossellini, the early De Sica, Fellini, and many others when he encourages realist filmmakers not only to depict reality but also to analyze it, study it, and even suggest means of modifying it. None of this would be likely to happen if the medium addressed itself only to a cinematic image that differed not at all from the images we get in ordinary perception. By showing us the world in the multiple ways that moviemakers cultivate as artists and through all the varied techniques to which they have access, film enables us to discover and enjoy features of reality that might have remained unnoticed. Even at this late date, the luminous *novelty* of the photographic image startles us. Why? Because it breaks the bonds of habitual perception and what psychologists call sensory accommodation.

In their unswerving emphasis upon the surface of physical reality, the realists fail to appreciate a whole gamut of visual effects that they seem to dismiss a priori on purely doctrinal grounds. Roemer, for instance, admits that the surrealistic nightmare images of Professor Borg in Bergman's *Wild Strawberries* are employed skillfully and with conviction, but then he rejects them because they do not show the material surfaces of everyday experience: "They are not true film images, derived from life and rendered in concrete, physical terms."[3] One would have thought, however, that the skillfulness of

Bergman's directing consists in his ability to go beyond the limits of the concrete and physical. Particularly if we place this sequence in the context of the entire film, we must applaud its inspired, and wholly cinematic, use of surrealist effects. The movie deals with the process of what Freud called the unconscious rising into consciousness. It is one long exploration by Professor Borg into damaging facts about himself that he has kept hidden from himself throughout his life. Now, as he approaches death, they finally erupt into conscious awareness.

Bazin, too, suffered from unfortunate prejudice against allowing the camera to convey symbolic or extrarealistic meaning. His attack on the technique of montage is motivated by his belief that it must always be unfaithful to the spatial continuity within our experience of reality and therefore necessarily unfilmic. He admires the works of Renoir because he thinks they are constructed out of "the skin of things": "this marvellous sensitivity to the physical, tactile reality of an object and its milieu; Renoir's films are made from the surfaces of the objects photographed."[4]

In chapter 6 I will try to show how greatly this interpretation misconstrues the genius of Renoir. Bazin goes wrong because he ignores the fact that Renoir treats physical reality as the setting and even revelation of human values that cannot be understood solely in terms of the outer aspects of the visual world.

As an anticipatory illustration of what I am referring to, consider the hunting scene in *The Rules of the Game*. Despite this film's occasional use of montage, Bazin extols its naturalistic flow and dispassionate delight in

the surface appearance of real objects, including the bodies of pitiful birds and rabbits being killed. But this
component of Renoir's talent does not fully explain his
achievement as a filmmaker. The hunt functions for him
not only as a demonstration of physical realities but also,
and more important, as an adumbration of slaughter
among human beings—both in World War II, which
began shortly after the film was made, and in the plot
itself.

When André, the aviator, is shot in the woods at the
end of *The Rules of the Game,* we are told that he fell
"comme une bête" (like an animal). Without the hunting
sequence, that partly visual, partly literary metaphor
would not have had the meaning Renoir wished to employ. Though we can recognize this only after seeing the
hunt, that is why Renoir wrote it into the script and
presented it at such length. The hunt operates as part of
his exploration into the social and interpersonal problems that mattered to him. Far from being a recording
of the outer aspect of a physical event, the sequence
attains aesthetic significance through its relevance to
extraphysical and extravisual dimensions of the drama.
In Renoir's presentation it has a conceptual role, albeit
one that is accomplished through its sensory appearance.

This brings us to the third of the four theses I mentioned
in chapter 1. The notion that film is a visual art that
depends on percepts rather than concepts follows from
the previous theses. It is also held independently by
theorists and critics who may not subscribe overtly to all

of them. While the battle over sound in cinema has long since been resolved and few people nowadays would agree with Arnheim when he laments that talkies deflect one's attention from the image on the screen, many writers still believe that since film is a visual art all other effects, including the conceptual, must be subordinated to the visual.

If one begins with that idea, one obviously assumes the filmmaker is an artist who needs highly developed visual powers. This suggestion is innocuous enough, but theorists have often concluded from it that the art of film requires few intellectual capabilities other than those that are immediately assignable to the visual. An inference of that sort is not at all innocuous.

Though they have been flattered by the possibility that they may be artists in a class with Michelangelo, Rembrandt, or even Shakespeare and Beethoven, and in fact that theirs may be the only living art that still flourishes in the twentieth century, most filmmakers are embarrassed when a stray philosopher claims that they should be respected as "thinkers." Knowing how demanding are the specialized needs of their visual art, they prefer to define themselves as workaday technicians, men and women whose expertise consists in observing the real world, looking through the camera, watching and advising actors in motion, editing celluloid in the cutting room, and then scrutinizing the total product when it is finally projected before them.

If one takes this attitude toward photography and film, one inevitably slips into the kind of view that Santayana enunciates when he separates photography

from the "ideal" arts. By their essence cinematic
creations would have to get their prime aesthetic value
from percepts rather than concepts, from remembrance
and reenactment of visual experience rather than
interpretation of the human condition, from visual
pleasures rather than the conceptual elaborations of
feeling or intelligence.

This dualism manifests itself most sharply in common distinctions between film and the literary arts.
Where the latter depend on words and abstract signification that only symbolizes the world it represents, the
former is thought to yield an experience that fascinates
and delights because it is immediately perceptual. In his
book *Novels into Film*, George Bluestone invokes this
dichotomy in order to explain why it is that few great
novels have been successfully adapted into films.

While he realizes that novelists often try to make the
reader *see*, Bluestone distinguishes between alternate
kinds of seeing. The first pertains to film or photography; the other occurs in literature: "One may . . . see
visually through the eye or [else] imaginatively through
the mind. And between the percept of the visual image
and the concept of the mental image lies the root
difference between the two media."[5] Further on,
Bluestone states that films come to us "directly through
perception" in contrast to the way in which language
relies upon "conceptual apprehension." He considers
this a difference not only between modes of experience
but also between ways of "apprehending the universe."[6]

In the history of film aesthetics there have been various modifications of Bluestone's approach. Purists have

claimed that film betrays its own essential mission to the extent that it even seeks to be literary, either by adapting works of literature or by introducing nonvisual concepts. On the other hand, many theorists have praised Bazin's attempt to defend "mixed cinema" by arguing that the medium's fundamental interest in the outer surfaces of the visual world does not prevent it from making adaptations of literary works if some filmmaker so desires.

All the same, Bazin and his adherents agree with the purists in affirming the basic difference between the two types of seeing. Bazin thinks that filmmakers can use a novel as their point of departure, but he also claims that the outcome will succeed only if they strip away everything that cannot be directly perceived in terms of physical appearances. This is the belief that seems to me unacceptable.

I do not wish to deny that films become inferior when they are overly talky, or when they are verbally discursive instead of using images to further the action, or when their eagerness to be "intellectual" makes them oblivious to the visual character of their medium—as in a filmed lecture that does little more than show us a man or woman uttering sounds. But there is nothing in the visual that necessarily excludes the conceptual, and therefore nothing that precludes a harmonization between percepts and concepts or between cinematic and literary effects.

Employing different materials as they do, the arts of film and literature have individual proclivities that must be acknowledged if authentic harmonization is to occur. But in great works of art the difficulties that this involves are readily surmounted, even turned to advantage, and usually because technicians in one medium have learned how to appropriate aesthetic opportunities encountered in the other medium. When T. S. Eliot argued for the use of "objective correlatives" in poetry, he was, in effect, requesting a merging between literary concepts and the imagistic percepts that are native to all the visual arts. In a similar vein, we can start at the opposite end and predict that images will be richer and more meaningful if they have conceptual implications like those that generally structure a poem, a play, a novel, or an epic.

The concepts in a film need not be identical with any that existed in the novel from which it may have been adapted, just as literary versions of the same myth do not have to duplicate one another. In creating their work of art, filmmakers should, and must, feel free to rely upon their own ideas about the subject matter they have chosen. They are not making, they cannot make, an exact translation, and their medium is sufficiently unlike literature to justify any number of alternate, yet equally valid, transformations. But if they approach a film with the assumption that it can scarcely benefit from conceptual exploration, or that the camera is incapable of developing quasi-literary ideas, or that proper dedication to technique rules out the possibility of extravisual insights, they cripple themselves unnecessarily.

As I mentioned, several of the theorists I have been criticizing admit that film need not limit itself to the outer skin of perceptual reality. Far from narrowing their goals to the portrayal of material factualities, many realists have wanted to abet political movements that would change these factualities. In his writings as a film critic, Bazin often shows how the best films reveal the human meaning in the scenes they photograph. But according to Bazin, as well as Zavattini and the others, this meaningfulness comes out of physical reality itself. They thought it could not be invented by the filmmaker; he or she would have to discover it by choosing selectively from the immanent significance that is already a part of the world.

What we are never told is how such meaning got into the world in the first place. In themselves material objects and physical processes are just brute occurrences in nature. If they acquire meaning it is because they have been fitted into the categories of thought and feeling that pervade, even define, our consciousness. The world makes sense to us only as we assemble, deploy, and rearticulate the diversified appearances in one or another system of ideation that is characteristic of the human species. Filmmakers who think they just look through the camera and do nothing but observe what is already meaningful in the given percepts they discover are simply deluded about conceptual presuppositions that they have introduced unawares, or else inherited from other people. These embedded concepts will not enrich a filmmaker's art as they might if he were able, at some level of his being, to understand what they are and how they have arisen in him.

For this aesthetic attainment to exist, there must be intellectual analysis and synthesis. It is based on the artist's capacity to master ideas in accordance with the needs of his own imagination. For a maker of movies, this means accepting and appreciating film as a partly conceptual art, an art that is always mixed insofar as it is reducible to neither concepts nor percepts in their purity. A great filmmaker is more than just a great technician of the visual. He or she must also know how to express values and beliefs that matter deeply to many people. In no other way can the transformations that constitute the art of film communicate to its human audience.

Cinematic meaning can be studied from the vantage point of different ideological approaches. Since I am not writing a commentary on prevalent film theories as such, I can freely bypass many of the challenging suggestions made by writers who identify themselves with Marxist, psychoanalytic, or feminist aesthetics. Some of the proposals offered by Christian Metz are nevertheless worthy of special attention in relation to what I have been saying about film as more than merely visual.

In his attempt to analyze the nature of film experience, Metz adopts Jacques Lacan's speculations about "the Imaginary" stage in a child's development. At some time in their first and second year, Lacan tells us, human beings achieve a sense of their individuality through an act of identification with the image of themselves that they see in a mirror. According to Lacan, this mirror experience gives the child a feeling of wholeness and unity, since it sees its body as a total something, and that initiates the belief in its selfhood and autonomy which continues throughout the rest of life. The mirror image being only a fictional representation, however, Lacan claims that it fosters illusory notions about the self and its separation from others. Originating in this primal confusion, the Imaginary then contributes to psycho-dynamic problems that everyone must deal with in later experience.

Metz accepts these ideas and thinks they explain our normal response to film, which he defines as a "play of presence and absence." The objects and events in a movie are known to be absent, only a screen being in front of us, but we submit to the feeling that they are somehow there in the photographic images that are actually present. Metz interprets this phenomenon, which he considers illusory, as a highly symbolic reenactment of the mirror experience that we had as young children and have been trying ever since to resolve through mechanisms of the unconscious. The Imaginary is presumed to operate in the phenomenology of film much as it did in the early encounter with a mirror. Metz believes that this explains why we see movies as unitary and continuous although they are really concocted of disjointed and often disconnected visual elements. He even claims the cinematic spectator can feel that he or she *is* the subject in the projected images. As in the mirror stage, the Imaginary engenders these and other illusory aspects of our response to film.[7]

In my opinion, theorists who hold conceptions such as these have been misled by false ideas about the nature of visual imagery. For one thing, neither mirror images nor photographic images are inherently illusory. Though it is difficult to know exactly what anyone perceives during the first year of life, we have no grounds for asserting that the initial acquaintance with mirrors creates radically mistaken impressions about the images they provide. As in later stages, one-year-olds may be said to "identify" with the image that appears in the mirror, and this identification may help them to realize that they are a single something just like the figure they are looking at. But what the child perceives is a two-dimensional object that resembles itself. Without that awareness, he or she cannot treat the mirror *as* a mirror. At no point does the child need to assume that it and the mirror image are indistinguishable. It must know that things it has already seen in the world, many of which are people of varying sizes, are not the same as itself. What the child now learns from its mirror image is that it, too, as a particular person, is also unified in its bodily structure. From this the child intuits that it is separate, even autonomous, within itself. That is not an illusion; that is the truth.

Nor is our perception of cinematic images ordinarily illusory. We are rarely deluded about reflections on the screen, even when we become so greatly absorbed in them that we have feelings that are similar to those we would undergo if we were indeed deceived. The shock, anxiety, tenderness, or revulsion that we may feel while watching a movie, carefully crafted to instigate these or comparable reactions in us, do not signify a cognitive distortion on our part. They are an overt response to what is being portrayed or expressed by the images, and they usually indicate that we have understood the meaning of these images. Far from our being fooled by photographic appearances, artificial though they may be in any of their frames or in a conjunction of disparate shots, our emotional attitude—provided it is relevant to the presentation—manifests an ability to experience the art form as it really is.[8]

This ability, like the ability to identify a mirror image as an image of oneself, may not be innate. But it is quickly learned. In any event, we have no reason to conclude that the mirror and the film experience are either identical or dialectically interactive in that mysterious realm called "the unconscious." An explicit image of ourselves appears in a mirror. That does not happen on the movie screen. We may say that something "in us" is presented there, or that as spectators we put a great deal of ourselves into our understanding of what we see, or that despite its being make-believe a film can show us what we really are. But these ascriptions, all of which require further analysis, should cause us to look for a new, and more plausible, theory of what it means for something to be imaginary. The one that Metz offers is not very useful.

As I have argued in other places, the imaginary is a branch or region of imagination.[9] The latter is the faculty by which some organisms, not all (as far as we can tell), entertain possibilities; the former deals with possibles in a special way that is definitive of itself. In ordinary language we often refer to imaginary conditions or events. Through the imaginary we construct the idea of fictionality, of unactualized possibles and even impossibles that can never be actualized. We recognize them as either logically or empirically incapable of being realized.

We have no idea of what it would be like for anything to be literally a round square, simultaneously both round and square as these words are colloquially used. But if in a lyric outburst a poet tells us that he or she *feels* like a round square, the imaginary arranges for us to make sense of this utterance. We could not have deciphered its meaning in any other way. Since round squares cannot exist, one might have said, nobody can feel like a round square, and therefore the poet must have been talking nonsense. The imaginary is the part of imagination that permits us to escape this difficulty. It is the means by which we understand impossibles as well as possibilities that cannot be actualized. Everything that is fictional issues out of this remarkable capacity that human beings have.

When the imaginary creates meaning in its distinctive manner, it imposes an ad hoc explication of what is being made intelligible. Finding no literal way to comprehend how even a poet could feel like something that is, by definition, impossible, the imaginary scans and then highlights alternative readings that might be coherent with the mentality of an "imaginative" individual. The adjective I have put in quotes refers to the fact that some people have a great ability to envisage possibles. As we say, they have a large imagination. The imaginary serves a reflexive and even self-conscious function: it is imagination using its aptitude for entertaining possibles to fathom how some impossibility can have meaning in and for a particular being or situation.

In the example I have chosen, this involves interpreting the poet as saying not that he or she feels what a round square *literally* does, for we cannot make sense out of that, but rather something else that is relevant to a person who makes such utterances. Through the imaginary we recognize that since nothing can be both round and square at the same time the incompatibility of these properties renders unstable any attempt to combine them. We then surmise that the poet claims to have a feeling of instability that is different but metaphorically equivalent. That is a possible we can understand.

This mental process, much more intricate than I have shown, can include vast leaps of imagination when the imaginary probes far afield for vivid illustrations that help it give meaning to what is literally impossible. In the creative work of highly imaginative people, these metaphoric constructs are a frequent and even standard mode of communication through the imaginary. Without the imaginary aspect of imagination, art could not exist.

In film the imaginary operates by using techniques that present things, persons, situations that are unreal or impossible and yet infused with such great intelligibility that we feel we are seeing a faithful representation of what is real. Filming a conversation between two characters who are looking at each other, Hitchcock's camera often positions itself behind the one who is speaking at that moment, instantaneously moving back and forth to focus on the face of the one who listens and is not speaking. In reality people who are conversing cannot put themselves in each other's position in this literal fashion. But through the imaginary we have no difficulty either discerning the cinematic relationship or detecting the meanings that Hitchcock develops through it. We realize that he is expressing the fact that as a conversant one sees the other person only from one's own point of view, but that both know they are engaged in having a communicative exchange, which the camera presents by filming their sequential involvement as speaker and as listener. If we are especially imaginative, we may relish Hitchcock's talent for conveying meaning through technical maneuvers of this sort. But even if our imaginative powers have not advanced to the degree that is requisite for this awareness, the imaginary enables us to understand what is happening on screen.

In itself the imaginary in film is more or less the same as for any other medium. In every deployment of aesthetic imagination there will be a similar creation of meaning through a delving into what is possible whether or not it can be actualized and regardless of the literal sense its metaphoric usage presupposes. And in each art form the imaginary meaning that eventuates will always depend upon the techniques through which the medium unites the artist's imagination with that of the audience.

These ideas about the imaginary reinforce my suggestion that film is best approached as a transformational art. Being reality transformed by the photographic images that process the real through their indigenous format, so too is film a transformation of visual and auditory possibilities into a coherent and intelligible totality resulting from the imaginary element of imagination.

To think that the imaginary is explicable in terms of the mere having of images, as Metz and many others do, is to misunderstand not only the imaginary but also the nature of imagination itself. Metz compounds this fundamental error by following Lacan in linking the imaginary to an alleged experience with mirror images in early childhood, and then forcing all subsequent encounters with the photographic image upon a procrustean bed that may be suitable for some of them but not for many, and surely not for all.

It is *because* the imaginary eludes the arcane contortions implicit in the Lacan-Metz theory that film is rarely illusory. Far from being deceived by the images on screen that intrigue us so much, we see them as meaningful emanations of whatever cinematic procedures have been chosen by the filmmaker. We are joined with him or her in an excursion within the imaginary. Having learned the rules laid down for this adventure, we quickly acquire the interpretive skills needed to experience the new reality that is the meaningful film we are watching. In addition to the realities it represents, we see it as a reminder of the life we have had in the past and in the present. These are different transformations. But neither they nor the other kinds result from a single or archetypal form of visual imagery.

The relevance of these remarks will appear in my critical analyses of two films, Visconti's *Death in Venice* in the following chapter and Renoir's *The Rules of the Game* later on. Bazin ascribed Renoir's importance as a director to his ability to "reveal the hidden meanings in people and things, without disturbing the unity natural to them."[10] I think this judgment is accurate, but scarcely coherent with Bazin's realist aesthetic. Visconti, who served an apprenticeship with Renoir, used the camera in ways that were sometimes similar. But though

Visconti's film is visually very beautiful, it is often prob-
lematic and unsatisfying. Its imperfections manifest
confusion about the surface of its visual images. Visconti
fails, to the extent that he does fail, because he refuses
to delve into ideas that exceed the perceptual brilliance
of his movie, whereas Renoir succeeds because he
continually probes the ramifications of fruitful concepts.

Death in Venice is an adaptation of a literary source.
The Rules of the Game does not purport to be an adaptation. But that is not a prime consideration. More significant is the separation between percept and concept,
the visual and the literary, since this causes the debility
in Visconti's film. Their harmonization gives Renoir's
masterpiece its lasting power.

In a magnificent montage near the end of the film, Visconti inserts a close-up of Tadzio's head, his face serene and his hair radiant, flaring, like the sun that symbolizes Apollo in mythology.

4

Death in Venice

For sight is the most piercing of our bodily senses; though not by that is wisdom seen . . . —Plato, *Phaedrus,* 250

Visconti's film is worth studying because it exemplifies so clearly the notion that cinema makes visually present to us aspects of reality that novels merely describe. Even at their most graphic, portrayals in a work of literature are effective only as they encourage the reader to imagine a scene or event, which he or she may never have experienced. The result must always be uncertain, though out of this uncertainty there arises that opportunity for conceptual inventions that enable fiction to tell us about the world. On the other hand, films may seem to *give* us reality through their visual concreteness. As I have been suggesting, more than that is required for a film to communicate not only the ideas of a novel but also a cinematic representation of them that is meaningful in itself. However we characterize the differences or similarities between visual and literary arts, their individual modes of transformation become particularly evident in films that are based on novels.

I am led to these reflections by the aesthetic strengths and weaknesses in Visconti's adaptation of Thomas Mann's novella, and by the possibility that some of them may be related to the filming of novels in general. Since 1971, when it appeared, various critics have expressed disaffection toward this movie, and therefore I will begin with its successes, a series of visual effects that—for me, at least—go a long way toward overcoming its failures.

First, however, I must quote from a passage in Mann's story that has mainly been ignored even though it is absolutely central to the author's intention. This fact alone is worth dwelling on, for surely so important a statement in the text should have impressed itself upon all critical readers. If it has not done so, perhaps that is because it tries to depict something that can hardly be shown in words. What it describes must be seen. An inspired filmmaker is needed to present its ideas vividly and with an immediacy that causes greater comprehension. The passage runs as follows:

There can be no relation more strange, more critical, than that between two beings who know each other only with their eyes, who meet daily, yes, even hourly, eye each other with a fixed regard, and yet by some whim or freak of convention feel constrained to act like strangers. Uneasiness rules between them, unslaked curiosity, a hysterical desire to give rein to their suppressed impulse to recognize and address each other; even, actually, a sort of strained but mutual regard. For one human being instinctively feels respect and love for another human being, so long as he does not know him well enough to judge him; and that he does not, the craving he feels is evidence.[1]

I have used the translation of H. T. Lowe-Porter. The one by Kenneth Burke does not read as well, but it ends with a line that captures Mann's basic insight: "For one person loves and honors another so long as he cannot judge him, and desire is a product of incomplete knowledge."[2] The entire fiction is constructed from this perspective, desire growing out of incomplete knowledge and that distance between human beings that results from the constraints of conventional behavior, but also from the danger of making contact, the elusiveness of consummation, and the unlikelihood of love.

Though Mann is able to use and develop these ideas throughout the narrative, he cannot really make us see them. He cannot present them in a visual epiphany. It is hard to grasp the full dimension of any desire by just reading about it or learning its causal mechanism. We have to inspect the choreography of movements, on the seashore, on the boardwalk, in the hotel, in the elevator, in the streets, through which the ambivalent desire of these characters maintains both presence and estrangement. We have to see the faces of the two individuals, we have to watch their eyes as they examine one another across the void, we have to know minutely and in all the infinite detail of perception what exists in the intervening spaces, we have to observe their bodies as they nervously consort with material objects that help them effect the pretense of mental distance—newspapers they read or finger, cups brought to mouths in a purposive manner, chairs that are sat in just so. To *see the desire*, the invisible thread that joins them in their separation without words or the exchange of ideas, we must move back and forth within their visual field.

Toward this end, Visconti's camera slowly zooms in
and out, the protagonists contemplating each other and
then withdrawing to preserve the space between their
autonomous worlds. These rhythmic zooming shots establish an ebb and tide that invests us with a moving
image of affective consciousness. They implicate the
camera as an erotic go-between, a messenger, an obliging
servant as in so many courtly and romantic love stories.
The affective swelling back and forth links these displaced persons through a massive metaphor about the
nature of desire itself. The metaphor is active even in the
camera's projection of the introductory credits, which
lyrically augment and reach out to us from the distance
of a black, unknowable background. It is a rhythm that
merges harmoniously with the long panning shots that
gently move the eye across a room or a beach filled with
many things, each of them subordinate to the one object
(from which they also separate us) that has occasioned
the visual and erotic search.

Given this mode of articulation, this rhythmic com-
bination of the zooming and the panning shots unified
by the concept of desire at a distance, the movie can
readily dispense with the first section of the novella. Like
Wagner's *Tristan and Isolde,* which it resembles in many
ways, the film begins with a ship on water and ends with
the lover's death on land. The ship heaves forward with
an impulse of longing, the camera panning and zooming
across an expanse of sad and languorous beauty, the
adagietto from Mahler's Fifth Symphony reinforcing the
image of desire. It is music laden with appogiaturas,

leaning notes, each yearning for the next one with a melancholy gladness, sometimes lapping over it but without being wholly resolved. The sounds do not awaken desire but rather luxuriate in its futility. On a much higher plane they match the salon string music played to lull the appetites of the guests as they chatter in the hotel lobby, waiting for dinner to be served.

A different aspect of desire is expressed in the contralto movement from Mahler's Third Symphony, which dominates the brief period of happiness when Aschenbach is able to work. He sits at a table on the beach, watching Tadzio with paternal affection, translating his incomplete beauty into the completeness of beautiful sounds. As Aschenbach composes, we intuit the same mysterious plenitude that permeates the vocal interlude, sung to the words of Nietzsche's *Thus Spake Zarathustra:* "Doch alle Lust will Ewigkeit, / Will tiefe, tiefe Ewigkeit!" (Yet all desire wishes for eternity, / Wishes for deep, deep eternity!) This, too, is the music of longing, but now it hovers about a still center or stable focus instead of merely yearning, suggesting that the elusive goal may even satisfy our desire.

In the slowness of his panning shots and in his leisurely cutting, Visconti resembles Antonioni. But unlike Antonioni, who often uses the camera to show us how *empty* a scene can be, chilling our perception with a sense of visual nothingness, Visconti revels in the fullness and seductive quality of what he portrays. And he does so because the beautiful is what an artist like Aschenbach would naturally desire. The exquisite sights and sounds in this film do not function simply as divertissement for the senses or even as nostalgic mise-en-scène. They serve as the explicit means by which Aschenbach's love of beauty can be made present to us, and they convey—as nothing in Mann can—the poignancy of losing a world whose goodness Aschenbach was created to enjoy.

Visconti's difficulties arise when his camera is stymied about this goodness, either because it cannot fathom its meaning or because it does not know how to communicate it. Even the short scene of creativity on the beach seems too long, forcing us to hear out the contralto without providing enough visual development or dramatic insight. It is not separation the images must now reveal but instead the ideal goal that lures the artist onward. Walking across the line of vision, the boy strolls in a way that suggests the *misterioso* of the Mahler movement, while Aschenbach writes the very music we are hearing, or rather, overhearing. Tadzio here incorporates the muse, eliciting Aschenbach's powers of inspiration. But once we get the idea, we find that the camera has nothing further to tell us. It does not really understand the inner joy that makes this a moment of supreme value to Aschenbach.

At other times, Visconti's directing is hampered by limitations within the visual itself. For instance, consider the final scene. In Mann it takes the following form:

Once more, he [Tadzio] paused to look: with a sudden recollection, or by an impulse, he turned from the waist up, in an exquisite movement, one hand resting on his hip, and looked over his shoulder at the shore. The watcher sat just as he had sat that time in the lobby of the hotel when first the twilit grey eyes had met his own. He rested his head against the chair-back and followed the movements of the figure out there, then lifted it, as it were in answer to Tadzio's gaze. It sank on his breast, the eyes looked out beneath their lids, while his whole face took on the relaxed and brooding expression of deep slumber. It seemed to him the pale and lovely Summoner out there smiled at him, and beckoned; as though, with the hand he lifted from his hip, he pointed outward as he hovered on before into an immensity of richest expectation. And, as so often before, he rose to follow. (Pp. 74–75)

In the film we see Tadzio turn back, one hand resting on his hip, and we see Aschenbach watching him as he sits in his beach chair on the shore. But also we see Aschenbach stretch out his hand to the boy, which is a minor change though it adds a bit of unfortunate senti-mentality, and we see him in the process of actually dying, which alters the novella quite a bit. Mann mini-mizes the physical character of Aschenbach's death in order to heighten the symbolic import of his final encounter with the image of Tadzio. We know he is dying because the word *Summoner* indicates that the "pale and lovely" youth is now the angel of death, Tadzio at this point merging with its earlier incarnations as the stranger in the mortuary chapel, the old roué on the ship, the Charon-like gondolier, and even the pale, snub-nosed Neapolitan singer.

Far from having to provide a realistic account of Aschenbach's demise, the passage depicts Tadzio as both

Hermes leading outward to the oceanic immensities of
death and also Eros directing the soul toward an infinite
beauty. Since the text requires us to take the term *Summoner* metaphorically, and to accentuate the words *it
seemed to him* and *as though,* we may even wonder
whether Tadzio has actually beckoned to Aschenbach.
The dying man may have had a private fantasy, a subjective vision that gives an idle gesture a significance that
applies only to his own condition. We do not know
whether Aschenbach has seen or just imagined the
movement of Tadzio's arm, and it is crucial to Mann's
design that we cannot know, that we have no way of
finding out.

In the movie, the symbolic content of the ending is
both curtailed and diminished by Visconti's reliance on
the visual. He has Tadzio walk out to the water, stand
with his hand on his hip, and turn his torso slightly. We
then see him lift his hand and point toward the sun. It
is all beautifully paced, and the cerulean sea and sky, a
single expanse under the morning sun, may very well
suggest the immensity of richest expectation. But if we
look at the film apart from the novella, we cannot possibly understand the meaning of Tadzio's gesture. Is the
arm raised for no reason at all, which seems strange, or
is Tadzio communicating by means of it? We know
Tadzio is leaving Venice that day. Is he saying farewell
to Aschenbach? But he does not wave his hand. And
why should the boy point toward the sun? Within
Visconti's film, there is no answer to these questions.
Being unwilling or unable to suggest that Aschenbach
has imagined the boy's gesture, and therefore that it is

to be taken metaphorically, Visconti presents it as actually happening, as belonging to the same real world as everything else that preceded it in this film. But then we don't know how to interpret it.

I speak of this as a defect caused by Visconti's unjustifiable faith in the purely visual. But what if someone argues that the scene succeeds for those who have already read the novella and perceived the symbolism in it? I am not opposed to this kind of solution, for if we see the film in its relation to the book we achieve a stereoscopic enrichment that is not to be scorned. At the same time, we may also feel that a film should be complete in itself, that audiences should be able to experience it fully even if they do not know the text from which it was taken. That is not an unreasonable demand. And even if we remember the paragraph in Mann, we still have to ask why the boy points to *the sun*.

Tadzio does not do that in the novella; there he just beckons. In the book, however, though not in the film, we have long since encountered the Platonic doctrine of love searching for perfect beauty, and we know that in Plato the sun often signifies the Good or Beautiful as an ideal essence. For Mann the sun can also represent the contrary, for instance when he speaks of its capacity to dazzle the spirit and induce a fascination with sensory objects. As in much of his fiction, Mann uses the relationship between the ideal and the sensory as a fundamental principle in the narrative. It recurs in the film through the scattered dialogues in the flashbacks between Aschenbach and Alfred, a fellow musician. After taunting Aschenbach at the beginning for failing to accept the ambivalent unity between the ideal and the sensory, Alfred reviles him later on for having destroyed his talent and touched bottom through the depravity of his submission to the sensory. This would seem to be the complexity of meaning that Visconti wanted to resolve in the last scene. But to decipher what he offers, we have to draw upon information that is available only to a student of Mann's writings.

Something similar occurs in Visconti's handling of the Esmeralda theme. At one point, after his infatuation has taken hold, Aschenbach comes upon Tadzio sitting by himself in a salon of the hotel and playing the piano. He is playing Beethoven's *Für Elise,* a composition often assigned to beginners on this instrument. The scene quickly evokes a flashback in which a much younger Aschenbach has just entered a brothel and hears the same music coming from an adjacent room. It is being played by a young and innocent-looking girl with handsome features not entirely different from Tadzio's. Though she is gentle and receptive to her client, she fails to satisfy him. We then see him make an unceremonious exit from the brothel, disgusted with himself and sexually frustrated.

The name of the girl is Esmeralda. The segment is taken from an event that occurs not in Mann's *Death in Venice* but rather in *Doctor Faustus,* a novel that he wrote some thirty-five years later. In *Doctor Faustus* the protagonist, who is a composer as in Visconti's *Death in Venice,* arrives in a strange city, asks a porter for the address of a modest inn, and is directed to what turns out to be a brothel. The young man, shy and unworldly, is horrified when he realizes where he is. He regains his composure only after he sees an unattended piano. When he touches its keyboard, he is able to cope with the reality of his situation. Before he can leave the brothel, however, he is accosted by the lovely prostitute, whom he spurns. At a later date, he seeks her out and has sexual intercourse despite her warning him that she has contracted a venereal disease. His subsequent infection becomes an important element of the narrative, since it may possibly be the source of his eventual madness.

The basis for this section of *Doctor Faustus* is a personal experience that Nietzsche describes in a letter. He writes about his having been misdirected to a brothel, his having frozen with consternation until he noticed a piano in a corner of the room, his striking notes on it that helped him escape. Some scholars, assuming that Nietzsche probably returned to the brothel, think he might have contracted there the syphilis often cited as causing his later dementia.

Writing fiction, Mann is free to use these biographical details as he wishes. He supplements Nietzsche's account by inventing the young prostitute, whom the protagonist calls Esmeralda and whose name he employs as a musical icon in one of his larger compositions. Selectively choosing from *Doctor Faustus*, Visconti has the girl fondly rub her forearm on Aschenbach's cheek, just as Esmeralda does with the composer in Mann's novel. The playing of *Für Elise*, and the intimation that

Aschenbach's lovemaking at their first meeting was emotionally disastrous, is Visconti's own contribution.

In the film we are left with the idea that Aschenbach's attraction to the beauty of Tadzio, who reminds him of Esmeralda, is also unwholesome and ultimately diseased. In Mann as well as Visconti, Venice itself appears as both an embodiment of beauty and a harbinger of deadly sickness. To communicate this concept, Visconti shows us the name of the ship that brings Aschenbach to Venice. On its prow, as it glides into port, we read the word *Esmeralda*.

Through visual metaphors such as this one, Visconti directs our imagination to what is pertinent in Mann's thinking about beauty, art, and death. In *Doctor Faustus* Mann even describes Esmeralda as "snub-nosed." But though Visconti's use of all this enhances the potential suggestiveness of his film, it can succeed only with an audience that is already cognizant of Mann's preoccupation with such problems. Does a filmmaker have a right to expect scholarly sophistication of this sort? Alluring as Visconti's images are, do they have sufficient meaning in themselves? And are they adequately integrated with the further meanings that Visconti obviously cares about but can only approach through our prior, and partly extraneous, acquaintance with Mann's literary output?

I pose these questions because difficulties arise each time Visconti departs from his source, changing it in ways that often have important consequences. Making Aschenbach a composer, and possibly a fictionalized

Mahler, is one of the glaring alterations. Purists who think that movie versions of literature must not deviate to this extent will always feel offended. But perhaps they tend to ignore what benefits a film and makes it into a separate artwork. It is only of secondary interest that Mann may have drawn the plot for his novella from something Mahler told him on a train coming back from Italy about an affair of his in Venice, or that Mahler's death a few months before the story was written greatly affected Mann, or even that he gave Aschenbach physical features that resemble Mahler's. What matters more is the similarity between Mahler's terminal romanticism forever saying farewell to life and Visconti's fixation upon images that seem to be arrested within their own beauty and therefore dead.

In producing these visual correlatives to death, whether in Venice or on the Lido, Visconti's camerawork is often outstanding. Moreover, with Aschenbach as a composer, Visconti can provide a narrative substratum that unifies the musical elements of this film, a noteworthy achievement in view of the role that music has in it. By having Aschenbach conduct his own compositions, Visconti can freely modify the linear structure of the novella through flashbacks that are dramatic and tumultuous. If Aschenbach had remained the writer that Mann depicts, we could have seen scarcely more than a man's back as he scribbles in his study.

Some of the other changes are less felicitous. For instance, Visconti has decided to give Aschenbach a still-living wife. We see her in some of the recent flashbacks, including one that immediately precedes his convalescent trip to Venice. On a table in the hotel room Aschenbach has placed her photograph, which he kisses. But we learn very little about her, and virtually nothing about their young daughter, whom we see at play with her parents in one flashback and being carried in her coffin in another. Mann mentions that the wife died after she and Aschenbach had enjoyed "a brief term of wedded happiness," and he casually remarks that the daughter is now married.

Modifications in these details accompany the flashbacks Visconti includes as meaningful analogies to some mood or feeling that Aschenbach experiences during his stay in Venice. In one of them his momentary joy flashes back to a scene that shows him romping in the mountains with his wife and daughter; in another his sadness issues into a memory of himself mournfully following the casket of his dead child.

Watching these flashbacks, we have the feeling that Aschenbach is a man who has known the joys and sorrows of marriage, more deeply than Mann suggests, and within a wider gamut of human emotions than appears in the novella. In making this variation, however, Visconti neglects the sentence that Mann puts at the end of his description of Aschenbach's family life: "A son he never had."

Within the structure of the book this becomes a pervasive theme. At the beginning, at least, Aschenbach's feeling toward Tadzio is mainly paternal. It is significant that the polite and well-ordered family to which Tadzio belongs, and for which Aschenbach acquires the concentrated obsessiveness that finally leads to his destruction, has no father—at any rate, none who is ever mentioned. Once Aschenbach receives reliable information about the cholera epidemic, he is in a position to save the family, and thus to carry out a paternal role. In failing to warn them, he proves himself a bad father.

For Mann this failure serves as a climax to the drama, revealing the extent to which Aschenbach's desire has become morally diseased. Afraid that he will lose sight of Tadzio, Aschenbach forfeits the possibility of family happiness—even with this surrogate family—and does not communicate as a loving father with that son he never had.

In the film little of this comes through, even though the principal events are reproduced. By showing Aschenbach engaged in scenes of family life, which we observe at moments of intense emotionality, Visconti changes the nature of his despair. It becomes the loneliness of one who has lost what he loved, instead of the loneliness of a man who realizes too late that he has never truly loved at all. Moreover, the flashbacks impede even this variation, for they are troublesome in themselves. Why does Visconti insert memories about the death of the young daughter where they appear in the film? Are they truly correlative to Aschenbach's depressed feelings at that moment? Does Aschenbach identify his daughter with Tadzio? Should we be thinking of the death of Mahler's children? And so on. The questions raised in us quickly become unmanageable and aesthetically unsettling.

Most of the other flashbacks connect Aschenbach's striving as an artist with his situation as a person who degrades himself in Venice. For instance, an early flash-back occurs shortly after Aschenbach sees Tadzio trudg-ing through the sand with his friend Jaschiu, who squeezes his shoulder and abruptly kisses him on the cheek. Aschenbach takes this as much more than casual effusion, and in the subsequent flashback we see him arguing with Alfred about the conflict between spirit and the flesh. Alfred claims that only through immersion in the senses can beauty be attained. As against this, Aschenbach insists that beauty is purely spiritual and can be apprehended only by an artist who pursues it through intellect and formal discipline. The issue having been posed, we then return to Venice and learn that Aschenbach has suddenly decided to leave. We have been prepared for this by Alfred's remark that Aschenbach is a coward, afraid to seek beauty through the senses, incapable of embracing the ambiguities in life as a great composer would.

Technically, this flashback is poorly done. We find it hard to follow the abstract and rapid-fire comments, harder yet to relate them to the events on the beach that called forth Aschenbach's remembrance of them. Leav-ing this aside, however, it is instructive to notice how Visconti has adapted what he read in Mann. In the novella there is no debate, only a speech of Socrates, presumably from Plato's *Phaedrus*, about the artist's search for beauty. In the lines that Mann has given us, Socrates argues against the ideas of *both* Aschenbach and Alfred. He says that regardless of how the artist seeks for beauty he will never be able to reach his goal. To the extent that the artistic pursuit lies through the senses, it is "a path of perilous sweetness, a way of transgression, and must surely lead him who walks in it astray." If, however, an artist strives for beauty through a "return to detachment and to form," this also culminates in the abyss. As a reaction against its own rigorous formalism, it leads to intoxication and irrational desire, luring even "the noblest among us to frightful emotional excesses, which his own stern cult of the beautiful would make him the first to condemn" (73).

Quite obviously, Visconti had wanted the relevant flashbacks to represent the differences between the two paths of art. But he never suggests that both may be calamitous. In fact, he gives us no reason to think that he himself has any opinions about the matter. In the novella, we do not know whether Socrates speaks for the author, and we are puzzled by the fact that the speech we read is not a copy of anything that can be found in Plato's dialogue. Mann has written a new version, relying perhaps on George Lukács's inaccurate interpretation of the *Phaedrus*.[3] Mann thereby awakens in us questions about his own beliefs. Is he glorifying or condemning, extolling or deploring, Aschenbach's quest for beauty? Is he or is he not encouraging creative persons to immerse themselves in what Joseph Conrad called "the destructive element," as so many Romantics had advocated? Or is Mann only portraying a syndrome that threatens all art and sometimes creates a barrier to its final justification, an ugly but inescapable concomitant (like death itself) to the artist's love of life and beauty?

Earlier in the novella, the narrator says: "in almost every artist nature is inborn a wanton and treacherous

proneness to side with the beauty that breaks hearts"
(26). But is there no other kind of beauty? Does Mann
think that Aschenbach's response to the inborn tendency
is characteristic of virtually *all* artists? If the artistic
nature is a product of disease, as Mann had gleaned
from his study of Freud, must it always follow the two
hopeless paths he delineates in this passage? Even
Schopenhauer was not that pessimistic.

Through the irony and systematic ambiguity of his
literary style, Mann arouses these queries without allowing us to ascribe any single doctrine to him. His novella
mimics nineteenth-century romances that celebrate the
artist's quest for beauty even though it results in death,
but he consistently maintains a pretext of realistic verisimilitude and the stance of dispassionate observation.
This ambiguity adds to the conceptual resonance of his
writing, teasing us with incompatible ideas about the
author's philosophy.

In Visconti's film, the ambiguity has lost its potential
strength. The camera watches with patient sensitivity,
but it does not deliberate or expect us to do so. Those
questions about the narrator's intentions no longer make
sense. The visual, in its single-minded devotion to apparent reality, leaves no room for irony in this movie. We
are in a different universe, one in which the images
discourage reflection and preclude those ideational re-
verberations that make the novella so compelling. In
the flashbacks we can see and hear the controversy
between Aschenbach and Alfred, who even condemns
Aschenbach for not admitting that his music (like
Mahler's) is always ambiguous in its harmonal texture.

But Aschenbach's love of Tadzio is hardly elucidated in relation to this issue.

As a result, the film has nothing like the elastic interplay between drama and aesthetics that emanates from Mann's literature. Visconti would have done better to delete the discussions between Aschenbach and Alfred and to substitute a voice-over narrator who could have delivered Mann's (or Visconti's) ideas, much as Orson Welles does with the ideas of Booth Tarkington in *The Magnificent Ambersons.*

As my reference to Welles's movie would suggest, I am not saying that, by the nature of their medium, all films must rely upon the visual in the way that Visconti's does. But from his example, we may detect problems that every filmmaker must confront. Visconti approaches them as he does because he adheres to aspects of the real world that novelists often ignore. Among others, these involve physical gestures, movements of the body, expressions of the face; and almost inevitably, but also intentionally, one assumes, Visconti emphasizes homosexual details more than Mann's novella did. Though the book includes an orgiastic dream that the movie does not present as such, Mann retains his governing ambiguity by never intimating that Aschenbach's pursuit of beauty is ultimately sexual. Merely by limiting his descriptions, Mann can distract us from anything he does not wish to consider. Thus, when Aschenbach first sees Tadzio in the company of Jaschiu, we are told only that "the two walked away along the beach, with their arms round each other's waists, and once the lad Jaschiu gave Adgio a kiss" (32).

In the novella, Aschenbach wants to shake a finger at Jaschiu, so we know that he feels threatened by such behavior. But we do not *see* any of the three characters, and we are told nothing more about the scene. In the film, we notice that Jaschiu presses his body ever so slightly against Tadzio's, and we observe Aschenbach smile to himself in a look of coy but unmistakable embarrassment. This alone magnifies the sexual content, which immediately imposes itself upon the narrative. After the revelatory smile, we see the flashback in which Aschenbach's friend castigates him for failing to seek beauty through a forthright acceptance of the senses. Aschenbach responds by trying to flee Venice. In the novella he makes his abortive attempt because he cannot stand the climate, having felt ill after a walk through the city. In the film we must infer that he leaves because of fears about latent homosexuality.

One might say that this difference between the novella and the film simply proves that Mann and Visconti had different points of view. And to some extent, that is an ample explanation. The film and novella do not have to be identical in all respects. The different media themselves encourage, and partly determine, different perspectives upon the world. An artist's intentions cannot be wholly separate from the exigencies of his art form, if only because he knowingly chooses it rather than another, and so commits himself to a particular gamut of artistic consequences.

At the same time, each artist selects what is meaningful to him or her from among the possibilities made

available by some medium. Visconti's selections demonstrate a predilection for the visual, and in this case the
erotic, that all too often nullifies conceptual ramifications
that Mann was able to exploit.[4]

Two or three concluding examples will suffice. Near the
beginning of the story, Aschenbach sits in the lobby,
watching the Polish family for the first time. He has
lingered so long that all the other guests have already
gone in to dinner. Eventually Tadzio and his group also
go. Walking out, Tadzio *happens* to turn and "as there
was no one else in the room," the narrator says, his eyes
meet Aschenbach's. In the film there is no way of knowing that Tadzio just happens to turn at that moment, or
that his eyes meet Aschenbach's because no one else is
in the room. Like the final scene on the beach, this one
shows Tadzio at a distance and hardly any facial clues
can be discerned. We see that Aschenbach is the only one
remaining in the lobby, but we have no reason to think
that this is why Tadzio looks at him. On the contrary, we
instantly assume that the boy's glance is the expression
of a personal and possibly sexual interest. In striving for
greater fidelity to the original, other directors might have
used close-ups and demanded more communicative
acting. But then, of course, the novella could have been
falsified (in some other way) by these new contrivances.

In combining the visual and the erotic as he does,
Visconti draws us into the heavy-lidded romantic atmosphere that has always been resident in the movies.
When Aschenbach, alone and in the dark, utters his
banal "I love you," we are shocked not because he

belongs to the same gender as Tadzio, or because he is old and ill, but because we realize how much he has detached himself from the situations in which these words are usually spoken on the screen. Desire at a distance precludes physical connection. Instead of being titillated by some intimate contact between two people, as in so many other films, we now see love as a consequence of human isolation. That condition also belongs to moviegoing, as I will argue in the following chapter. We too are isolated as we sit in the darkened auditorium. We observe at an insurmountable distance entrancing images that may easily embody our desire but can satisfy it only aesthetically.

Neither Mann's novella nor any other work of literature is capable of duplicating this multiple effect. It issues from our experience of films as they have existed for almost a century, and in Visconti's—where language is muffled by an environment that structurally prohibits direct communication—we are shocked by the disparity between the consummate words we hear and the incommensurate realities that surround their utterance.

Weaving its imaginary web out of distance being shown as that which separates two human beings while also joining them through the filament of desire, Visconti's film draws upon the voyeuristic element in cinematic art. With one exception, and that is very casual, Aschenbach and Tadzio never touch each other. They just look, as we in the audience do in following the imagery that purveys their story. The narrative continuity mostly consists of successive occasions on which an elderly man and a fourteen-year-old boy keep watching each other, their relation being delimited by the barriers of age, nationality, family expectations, and the need to conform to social mores of Venice in 1911. These give this movie its organic unity, but voyeurism not too dissimilar exists in the experience of all other films—as well as all visual art, and possibly all craving by human beings to fixate and possess whatever they designate as reality.

My final illustration comes from the scene with the barber. This is how Mann describes Aschenbach's magical rejuvenation: "the oily one washed his client's hair in two waters, one clear and one dark, and lo, it was as black as in the days of his youth" (69–70). But how could Visconti be expected to ask Dirk Bogarde (Aschenbach) to dunk his head first into one basin and then into another? The visual appearance would doubtless have been unsightly, and the behavior too routine. Instead, the barber dips a brush into a bowl of dye and paints Aschenbach's hair, in long, graceful, loving strokes, and without washing it at all. There can be no question about the suitability of what Visconti has preferred, and in the slow rhythmic movement of the barber's hand as he applies the dye we can see a gesture that imitates Visconti's mobile camera throughout the film.

Actually, the camera remains stationary at this point. As the brush colors Aschenbach's hair, finally eradicating the distance between himself and that image of youth he has hopelessly desired, it just looks. But this serves to increase the effect, as if Visconti was now bestowing an egocentric tribute upon his own virtuosity. What has disappeared is the contrast between the clear and the dark. Through it Mann evokes the image of the two horses that Plato describes in the *Phaedrus,* the white one leading upward to a love of spiritual beauty while the black one drags the aspiring soul down toward the abyss.

In Mann we are free to take the clear and dark waters as just a trivial naturalistic detail; we *need* not see them as meaning what Plato had in mind. In the film the very possibility of these alternative interpretations has been abolished. And for some audiences, nothing will equal Visconti's failure to retain this conceptual value. To them it will seem as if he, like Aschenbach dazzled by the sun, has been blinded by the perceptual beauties that the camera keeps generating.

For others, however, Visconti will have redeemed himself by showing us the painted face and hair of Aschenbach, transformed into an embalmed, multicolored spectacle of his own death. In his account Mann had not gone that far. He himself may not have visualized the scene to this degree.[5] Without the film we might never have realized what the words of the novella imply but do not state. Nor could we sense, with the immediacy of sight, the identification of Tadzio with Apollo, the god of visual beauty and of art. In a magnificent montage near the end of the film, Visconti inserts a close-up of Tadzio's head, his face serene and his hair radiant, flaring, like the sun that symbolizes Apollo in mythology. Nothing comparable was available to Mann.

In one of the final scenes a photographer's camera stands abandoned on the beach like a piece of ineloquent statuary. It, too, appears in the novella; and some readers have thought that its tripod, which Mann mentions, is a symbol of the tripod at Apollo's Delphian oracle. In the movie the ancestral instrument represents the photographic art itself. Visconti's camera stares at it like a *frère semblable*. It is, in fact, another open eye (and possibly reminiscent of the sea-monster's eye at the end of Fellini's *La Dolce Vita*) through which the world may sometimes reveal itself while also hiding the manifold truths that sight alone cannot attain.

III

5

Communication and Alienation

In turning now to the last of the four theses, we see immediately its importance for the other three. Those who believe that film is basically a reproduction or recording of the visual world often cite its being the product of a mechanism, the camera. They treat this as sufficient reason to assert that cinematic art adheres to the "outer aspect of things," that it primarily concerns itself with duplicating physical reality, and that its domain is the perceptual rather than the conceptual.

The realist ontology of theorists like Santayana and Bazin accentuates the fact that photography is a product of *automatic* technology. From this they infer that the camera is a machine for capturing reality on its own and without further instructions. It is thought to be an automaton that processes visual appearances without altering them as, for instance, the art of painting does. Santayana concludes that if photography is to be considered an art form it is nevertheless different from any of the "ideal" arts, since they provide intentional transformations and creative reconstructions of the real world. Though he does not say so, Santayana implies that photography is a minor art. Its products being machine-made, he felt they could not match either the individual expression or the human responsiveness that one associates with the greatest achievements in painting, poetry, music, sculpture, and the like.[1]

As one of the principal creators of film aesthetics, Bazin finds nothing in the technology of the camera to render photography into a minor art. But like Santayana, he claims that the medium's tie to reality can only be understood by reference to its automatic operation. For him the "myth of total cinema," by which he means its underlying motivation, consists in the search for greater and greater approximations to reality by means of increasingly perfected developments in the camera. He portrays photography in general, and cinema in particu-lar, as evidence of humankind's obsession with a realism that even trompe-l'oeil painting cannot equal. The spec-tator of a realistic painting must always be aware that it was done by a painter's hand. Unlike the camera, the brush is not automatic machinery. While the realism of a work is jeopardized by our knowledge that a handheld brush was instrumental in its creation, Bazin maintains, cinema frees the human reality-search of all subjectivity: "Photography and the cinema . . . are discoveries that satisfy, once and for all and in its very essence, our obsession with realism [by means of] a mechanical re-production in the making of which man plays no part."[2]

Questions about whether photography is or is not a minor art need not detain us long. One recognizes that some valued activities are less creative than others, and therefore that some arts will have to be ranked as relatively minor. But this is not a very interesting problem. And even if still photography were indeed a minor art, that would not prove that the same is true of cinema. If only because it introduces a dynamic approach to space and time, in contrast to more static uses of the camera in still photography, film would have to be classified differently. In some ways, still photography is to the movies what lyric poems are to epics and what songs are to operas. Some people may wish to argue that the former are all examples of minor art. Others can surely maintain that size and complexity are irrelevant as far as aesthetic value is concerned. Here, at least, we need not try to resolve this kind of issue.

Of greater importance is our asking what follows from the fact that both photography and cinema depend on the automatic technology of the camera. Bazin believes that this dependency affords the possibility of liberation from subjectivity. That seems to me another confusion on his part. To begin with, it is not the mere reliance on technology that is at stake. The brush of a painter and the chisel of a sculptor are also forms of technology. They are not, however, automatic or mechanized in the way that a camera is. They must be guided at every moment by a human hand, itself an implement of a human mind that, looking before and after, decides how this part of our body shall be employed for the creation of each and every detail of the final outcome. In being programmed but not subjected to any such limitation, the camera—like the computer—would appear to have access to a kind of objectivity that no other art can equal. And in the sense revealed by the facts I have mentioned, this is true.

But the conclusions drawn by theorists like Bazin are much less plausible. Though the camera may not be held as a brush is, and often is not held at all, it, too, must be directed. Its automatic function requires an outlook beyond itself, an intelligence by which it is told *how* to capture reality. The camera is manipulated, ordered to provide an image that transforms reality by eliminating whatever a filmmaker considers detrimental to the work of art he or she brings into being.

In film this occurs most obviously through the varied methods of cutting and editing that pervasively define cinematic style; but within the photography of each frame there must also be a meaningful interpretation of what is being offered as the likeness of reality. Even automatic technology cannot show forth an epistemological given independent of our involvement. What people identify as real will always manifest their powers of recognition. For the filmmaker the camera is something to be looked *through* in order to see what one is looking *for,* and how one is looking for it. This constrains what the cinematic artist can do aesthetically, but it also yields new opportunities for expressing a complexity of feelings and ideas that are able to attain visual articulation.

In the service of a gifted cinematographer, the camera presents images whose meaningfulness is not reducible to either technology or automation. To this extent, film (and all other photography) resembles the types of "ideal art" that Santayana mentions. Filmmakers become creative artists by using their automatic technology to say in visual terms arresting things about the world, sometimes with words, sometimes without them, but usually through a conjunction of the two. The fact that a camera's mechanism is automatic does not make it metaphysically more objective. By itself and however improved in its operation, it can only give a camera's view of reality. The intentional transformations that Santayana rightly ascribes to fine art belong to the medium of film in its entirety, which includes but is not limited to the camera's technological capability. The filmmaker subjugates his or her reliance on automation by investing the photographic image with whatever meanings it is able to have.

As in the rest of art, these meanings are both affective and cognitive conveyors of interpersonal communication. They involve the feelings and the concepts by which men and women make their presence known, jointly struggle with problems in the environment, and share with one another consummatory experiences available through whatever sense modality. Because they involve the automatic technology of the camera, the aesthetic transformations that make cinema into an art form will differ noticeably from those one finds in other arts. But though we are beguiled by photographic realism, we nevertheless know it functions as a vehicle of imagination that subjugates even perfected automation. When Kracauer talks about the "formative" dimension of film, he seems to be referring to this radically creative element of filmmaking. What Kracauer has to say about it, however, contradicts much of what he previously claimed when he remarked that film, by its very essence, is a recording of reality.

In making these comments, I recognize that film art is an apotheosis of modern technology. Together with its colonization in television, video, and the monitoring of computer input, the cinematic revolution unleashed a power to communicate that marks a turning point in human development. Unless a worldwide catastrophe befalls us, our species will never revert to its dependence on the older means by which people used to exchange ideas or feelings with each other. This is not to say that the advent of film as our principal mode of communication will necessarily supplant the arts that were dominant before. On the contrary, they have already learned how to benefit from it. But in having an ontology predicated upon the technological advances that are distinctive of this moment in history, film will doubtless remain the most vital art form for many years to come.

Of course, the head that wears this crown must feel its heaviness. In having harnessed the potency of visual and auditory technology, cinema has also made a pact with the devil. So seductive is the vibrancy that film communication affords that we sometimes forget how thoroughly it induces a hidden and corresponding alienation. As even the earliest theorists remarked, we sit in the movie theater, or in our living rooms, watching on a screen pulsations of light that are unlike anything else in nature even when they register a faithful representation of the visual world.[3]

There are advantages to being isolated in this manner. It often enables us to communicate more efficiently than we could have done through less artificial means or in a personal conversation. The visual signifier disbursing meaning can now be packaged with extraordinary skill never achieved before. Irrelevant details are easily prevented from distracting us, and often they are eliminated entirely by the editing of the film itself. The consummatory quality of this applied technology encourages us to focus our attention in a way that we ourselves do not always notice. Without thinking about it, we correct for distortions in what we see while also warding off interference from anything that would lessen the marvel of cinematic absorption.

Yet all this comes at a price. In the midst of our new and wonderful experience we may not realize how less than wondrous is the effect of having our vision channeled by it. Though we communicate through film, it cannot banish an insidious distance induced by the situation itself. Having acquired the ability to enjoy values that film can offer, our species may be changing its sense of what reality is apart from these artificial transformations. I remember hearing an interview with a teenager who had met the president of the United States, at the time Jimmy Carter. When she was asked what he looked like, she replied: "Oh, much shorter than he really is." She meant much shorter than he appears on television; but that, obviously, was for her a more authoritative indication of his height than anything her own face-to-face awareness could accommodate.

Despite its own artificiality, a live production in a theater runs counter to this tendency. Watching actors on a platform, we see human beings pretending to be characters who are themselves human either literally or symbolically. In stage performances there is a responsive interaction between the actors and their audience that cannot exist in film. Far from being incidental or adventitious, this immediate exchange is part of the aesthetic transaction that constitutes the art of theater. That is why every enactment of a play is a different version of it, which is also the case with music in the concert hall. In these arts the bidirectional sensibility affects the nature of the product that emerges on each occasion. Playing music and acting on the stage are called "performing arts" because their artfulness consists in communicating back and forth through the performances themselves, at the time of their occurrence and as they are happening.

The communication that film affords is nothing of the sort. However natural a character in a movie may seem, however familiar to us the actor who portrays that character may be, we in the audience are conscious of being isolated from both the character and the actor in a manner and degree quite different from theatrical productions. Though we are not allowed to converse with live actors while they perform, we always know that we *could* do so, even if that meant violating the rules of this particular art form. But as members of a film audience, we cannot interact with either the performers or the characters, much as we might like to. Within our aesthetic experience we are alienated from them by the very technology that makes them imagistically present to us.

On the other hand, since there are no actual people on the screen, and therefore no possibility of disturbing anyone's performance, we may readily talk back to the photographic images that relentlessly entrance us in their emanation out of thin air. Thanks to the darkened privacy of the hall, we can also release our feelings surreptitiously, and perhaps more fully than we might if others were addressing or observing us. It is as if we compensate for the alienation built into the cinematic medium by allowing it to elicit responses that would be prohibited in our usual modes of interpersonal existence.

Phenomena such as audience involvement in *The Rocky Horror Picture Show* can be explained in a similar fashion. Interactive television helps us to overcome our remoteness by collaborating in the presentation itself. The *Rocky Horror* experience is a communal event in which aficionados prove their identity with one another by showing their joint devotion to everything, including all the spoken lines, that appears in the aesthetic vehicle. It is like the annual running of the bulls in Pamplona. Through interactive contributions to the artistic product, whether in television or CD-ROM, we establish ourselves as participants in a creative community. That alone may not eliminate the fundamental sense of isolation: we know that what we do is always compensatory and secondhand. But, at least, it modifies our separateness and reconstitutes the circumstances under which it occurs. Moreover, the history of cinema demonstrates that the residual sense of alienation can be smothered and ignored when audiences become habituated to it. They learn how to enjoy the results of being alienated. Whether the condition can be truly conquered remains uncertain.

Combining elements of communication and alienation, and then using them as central to its efforts as an art form, film confronts a dichotomy that is deep in human nature. However mistakenly, we tend to define ourselves in terms of our consciousness. That feels to us as if it were a totality unto itself. Though we are also our body, and by extension the realm of matter in which our body operates through physical processes that permeate nature as a whole, we readily think of materiality as something different from ourselves. The mind-body dualism, which has been so stupefying in Western culture (and so cognitively productive as well), arises from this common intuition. Our mind feels separate or detached from nonconscious entities, including our own body. Partly because of the shame and guilt that society imposes as a restraint upon our interest in matter, we gravitate toward living creatures, and above all toward those that have consciousness like our own. We treat them as the preordained objects for communication. Sensing our alienation from inanimate reality, we fear it as a destructive force that will eventually, in death, triumph over us.

Through technology this attitude is challenged and consecutively opposed. Whether or not technology delivers on its promise, it generally offers itself as a benign improvement upon nature. It, too, relies on physical and chemical phenomena, but it does so with the explicit purpose of serving life by magically providing satisfaction for almost any need a person might have. If you are bored, just flip on the television or pop in a videotape. If you feel diminished and defeated in your search for emotional fulfillment, just watch a romantic flick on the larger-than-life screen of your local movie house. This may even be more palliative than going to some other house of pleasure.

Film depends on technology more than any former art, but each generation has successively acquired increased ability to adjust to the cost it exacts in isolating us from the human world with which we might have communicated directly. The automated distance inherent in the film (or computer) experience can become a welcome escape from the recurrent, frequently intrusive, confrontations that saturate modern life. And in being a medium of artistic expression, film transcends the mechanical bases of its own techniques by using them to attain meaningful consummation. As in all art, it thereby creates a harmony of nature and spirit.

The dialectical interweaving of communication and alienation in film psychology has been studied by various theorists. F. E. Sparshott argues that "cinema vision is alienated vision." He explains this by saying that not only do we see on the screen a two-dimensional arrangement of a three-dimensional scene but also we undergo spatial ambiguity. Though all our other sensory cues come from our physical location in the theater, the visual character of film includes viewpoints that are not themselves related to our bodily presence but rather projected upon it. "It is the alienation of the visual sense in cinema space," Sparshott writes, "that makes possible many of the uses and special effects of film that work against its function as record."[4]

Jean Mitry describes the phenomenology of cinema more graphically when he says that, in watching movies, "I *know* myself to be in the theater but I *feel* myself in the world offered to my inspection . . . at one and the same time I am *in* this action and *out* of it, *in* this space and *out* of this space. Having the gift of ubiquity, I am everywhere and nowhere." Like Sparshott, Mitry treats that condition as definitive of cinematic art. This "equilibrium of contradictory effects is indispensable," he remarks. "On this instability rests the perfection of film."[5]

In his essay "The Work of Art in the Age of Mechanical Reproduction," Walter Benjamin suggests that reproductions diminish the presentness of the object or event being reproduced. He says that this was tolerated in earlier periods because the product had a function within some cult or ritual. In our age, according to Benjamin, film technology creates an alternate syndrome: "For the first time in world history, mechanical reproduction emancipates the work of art from its parasitical dependence on ritual. To an ever greater degree the work of art reproduced becomes the work of art designed for reproducibility."[6]

The question we should ask is whether this emancipation of the mechanical, occurring at its fullest as it does in the art of film, can ever manage to surmount the loss of presentness that results from reproduction. In this context the word *presentness* refers less to the reality of what is being copied or represented than to its affective accessibility. Because we feel at home with them, and above all if we care about them, real men and women are affectively accessible. We interact concretely on many levels, and often in ways that are both beneficial and enjoyable for us as well as them. People are present not only as realities we stumble over but also as persons who matter to us. Our emotional orbits overlap and, to some extent, we define ourselves in relation to each other's being.

Presentness of this type, entailing the ability to communicate on an interpersonal level, counteracts alienation or a sense of isolation. Can these be totally exorcised, or might they be worsened, by that reproducibility of the reproduction to which Benjamin refers? In our immersion in cinematic possibilities, are we experiencing a greater communication than was available in the past, or are we being more completely detached from the energies of life in nature?

The aesthetic transaction in film would certainly seem to be different from any that preceded it. And yet, one might reply, the filmmaker and his entire company perform with an imagined audience in mind, as artists have always done. Even highly narcissistic moviemakers direct their professional ventures toward other persons, with whom they may be covertly trying to communicate.

This can have its utility in every art. The poet Robert Graves once told me that writers should have a personal muse for whom they write. I have occasionally found that helpful in my own efforts as an author, and possibly something comparable occurs in all work that purports to be creative. If this is so, the mechanization that pervades, but is subdued by, cinematic inventiveness may only signify the risk of unilateral communication that each medium must run. In other words, the problem of alienation is neither insoluble nor unique to film.

At the same time, movie actors may well lament being constrained to make their fragmentary performances without any responsive audience before them while they create. That is something other performing artists do not have to face. And despite the engrossing vivacity of images on the screen, a film audience can be troubled by a similar lack of human immediacy. This effect is variable, of course. Just as small children sometimes cannot distinguish television commercials from recommendations made by their parents, neither do they find it difficult to believe they are in direct contact with the persons or animated beings portrayed in the movies they watch.

Adults have other ways of reaching across the distance that mechanization produces. In a question and answer session that I attended, Jack Lemmon said that, especially in the case of comedy, film actors must and do accomplish imaginative feats designed to cope with the loss of instantaneous reaction that accompanies a stage performance. In the scene of *Some Like It Hot* where Lemmon lies in bed and tells Tony Curtis that Joe E.

Brown has just proposed marriage to him, Billy Wilder suggested that he punctuate his account with a frenetic clacking of maracas in his hands. This worked perfectly in that scene because, as Lemmon explained, it helped him during the pauses in the dialogue to imagine a live audience responding to his delivery, even though he was being observed only by the camera staring impassively.

In his essay Benjamin refers to Pirandello's comment about a "feeling of strangeness" that invades an actor when he appears before the camera. Pirandello identified this feeling as the type of estrangement everyone experiences in looking at himself in the mirror. We can extend Pirandello's idea (so different from Lacan's) by imagining an actor who not only looks at himself but also performs in front of the mirror. That magnifies the sense of strangeness. If one looks at one's image in the mirror, one sees the face of someone who is *looking*, and doing so in this contrived manner. That, we rightly intuit, is not how we "really" look in life, since our natural appearance has now been violated, contorted, ossified into an unspontaneous self-presentation, and therefore rendered wholly artificial. But all art is artificial, and the actor's art entails a deliberate showing of himself. Why, then, does acting before the mirror induce even greater estrangement than merely looking at it?

I think the reason is that if one acts in front of a mirror one is inevitably acting *for* the mirror. But a mirror is not an audience; it is just an instrumental thing, an optical device. It has none of the affective responsiveness that living creatures have. Neither does the camera, and that is why film actors quickly learn that they must never act for *it.* In a documentary entitled *Acting in Film,* Michael Caine advises actors to forget entirely about the presence of the camera. They need only make their features and their movements available to it, he says, since a camera has its own method of putting these to use. If the camera likes what it sees, that's fine. If not, there is nothing an actor can do about it.[7]

Caine does not mention the man or woman who stands behind the camera and largely determines what it will like by telling it what to see. Nevertheless Caine's insights are pertinent to the question of estrangement on the part of the film audience as well as the participating actors. If you forget about the camera while performing, you are not tempted to act for it. So, too, does the mirror hang on the wall and carry out its prescribed function without your having to peer into it in the hope of finding what you really look like. Estrangement due to the automated nature of the films we see can be similarly controlled: we just ignore the causal origin of our experience and attend to the humanity that presents itself by means of it.

This kind of concentration belongs to the aesthetic interest an audience bestows upon the absent actors. It is the spectators' way of dealing with the inhumanity of a mechanized relationship. But *can* people obliterate their knowledge of what is being avoided? That would be like telling them not to think of an elephant. In the "back of their minds," to use that oddly spatial metaphor for a nonspatial reality, even the most seasoned professionals or most fully captivated members of the audience are aware that film is at the mercy of its technology, and to that degree a less than purely human medium.

Communication in and through the film experience is always a compromise, as much of art is, and most of life itself. Whatever communication there may be in film, it results from viable equilibrations with the materiality of the medium. Though the element of alienation can never be totally eradicated, we can live with it. Great films are those in which the problems created by this situation get resolved in a transaction that is inherently consummatory. No other criterion of excellence is needed.[8]

By recognizing the peculiar nature of communication and isolation in cinematic art, we may also be able to explain what it is to be a "star" in the movies. That concept is uniquely geared to the conditions we have been discussing. In other areas of life—in politics, in religion, even in different arts as they have developed in the last two hundred years—remarkable, often extremely charismatic, men and women have also received an adoration from large numbers of people who do not know them personally but put them in an affective class by themselves. Movie stars are different from the others *because* they symbolize the glamour of technological remoteness ingredient in their art form. Though they can be seen enlarged on the screen, and repeatedly in the same or different films, they cannot be approached in their mechanized ideality.

Like the heavenly bodies, the movie stars glitter from afar as entities that seem to have a being that eludes the mundane existence of either the personages they portray or the audiences that are transfixed by their portrayal.

Where saints, heroes, cult leaders, and epiphanies of some deity clothe themselves in the raiment of a moral or religious mission, the stars dazzle us just in being the evanescent persons who lend their splendor to whatever narrative they enter from one film to another. Descending from their distant galaxy, they outshine their appearances as fictional characters, whose names we immediately forget because they are experienced as little more than fleeting revelations of the glowing individuals who inhabit them.

This circumstance derives from our constant recognition that what we perceive in a movie is not just a photographic image. It is additionally a transformation of reality that elicits our strongest feelings without there being any possibility of reciprocation. We often communicate with one another by means of images, but we cannot communicate with images themselves. We cannot traverse the gulf that separates us from them. That would be like having a chat with the square root of -2. Renewing their presence in each image that conveys their meaning for us, the stars symbolize the endless repetition that each atomic frame enjoys when films are played over and over again. The title *The Eternal Return* that Jean Cocteau takes from Nietzsche (who meant something totally different) applies not only to the romantic ideology of the Tristan myth as adapted in that film but also to the eternal recurrence of the cinematic frames and whatever they embody.

In their adoration of the stars, fans attest to an insatiable love of the movies, and of the conditions that make them possible. The stars are idealizations of the infinite remoteness between us as transient beings and the unchanging icons created on the screen by the glory of film technology. Like the MGM lion, which is both natural and artificial, the stars are themselves works of art that reveal the astounding transformations we expect to find in film after film.

Because movie stars are idealized in this fashion, it is not surprising that a characteristic type of disappointment can issue from a glimpse of them as they actually exist, walking in the street like everyone else or waving to their admirers in a newsreel. Their stardom may seem sullied by those all-too-human persons pretending to be themselves as they get out of limousines prior to the latest world premiere. Though we love to see their indelible features, engraved in our minds like the outlines of hands or feet cemented in a Beverly Hills sidewalk, we sense their embarrassment in appearing unmistakably mortal. We intuit their uncertain desire for both the anonymity of private life and the sheer publicity of displaying themselves as luminaries in their own firmament.

Even famous stage actors do not affect us that way. Their mortality is more obvious. As we watch them in performance, we know that they can unexpectedly fail or succeed at any time. They are like boxers or astronauts, whose celebrity results from always living at the edge of danger. Film stars are exempt from any such peril, just as the gods and goddesses of religion are. The stars do not change their performance each time a film is played, though their characters and the quality of their acting can vary from film to film. As stars, they exist timelessly in the temporal art they make possible. They fascinate us because the world in which we have our being is so remote from that. Unless they are deluded by their own legend, the men and women who are movie stars may feel additionally estranged or alienated by their profession. More than anyone else, they know how much their stardom is a construction, like Frankenstein's humanoid, of other people's technology and manipulative imagination.

In one place Benjamin asserts that unlike painting at present, but similar to epic poetry in the past and architecture at all times, cinema provides "an object for simultaneous collective experience."[9] Contrasting film with painting, on the one hand, and emphasizing its kinship with epic poetry, on the other, seems right. But film differs from architecture inasmuch as film is an art that brings human beings together in order to have an experience of itself. Architecture is collective in another sense. It has its social effect by being a setting for whatever it is that people do in that location. Even when tourists visit en masse some palace or city square and jointly delight in its beauty, they know this architecture was originally constructed to vivify the life of those who live there. The tourists are present as a group, but they do not have the collective experience that architecture creates in the persons for whom it has a daily and pragmatic importance. In the art of film there rarely is a situation of that sort.

My saying this may seem counterintuitive at first. Going to the movies has always been a social activity, and in some communities the only one that involves all the menfolk or even all the families, complete with very small children, as still happens in parts of Italy and Spain. Nor can we deny that the content and artistry of great propaganda films, such as those of Leni Riefenstahl, are designed to elicit a mass response in the audience. Nevertheless, the difference between film and architecture remains, as illustrated even by these examples. It is one thing to hear Hitler at a rally in Nuremberg or Mussolini in the Piazza del Popolo. It is something else to see films that record their speeches. Though in the company of others doing the same, people in the film audience must always struggle with their individual distance from the mechanized art that transmits these historic events.

Being present simultaneously, the spectators of such films may all have a similar involvement with the realities shown to them on screen; and sitting together in the auditorium, they may have a sense of solidarity, even friendliness, with one another. But this mutual identification is derivative from the film experience that each has privately, whereas in architecture whatever oneness there may be emerges directly out of the human relations that create a unifying meaning within the communal life of some particular place.

The presentation of films is temporal, as it is for music. Though these can be recorded, even canned, they do not exist in any space and are not observable as spatial entities are in the real world. A movie, like a musical composition, begins at a moment in time and ends later on. Each has its being by moving *through* time. But a motion picture is also a picture of motion, which means that it portrays things and persons as *they* move through space. Since music is not a visual art, it cannot do that.

Over and above these differences between cinema and architecture or music, there is another reason to place film in a special aesthetic category. Unlike architecture and beyond anything music, even opera, can achieve, movies have a self-referential capacity that enables them to introduce into their narrative fabric those problems about communication and alienation that are relevant to the medium as a whole and that we have been discussing in this chapter. I can show this in more detail by analyzing *The Rules of the Game*.

Renoir refers to Dalio standing next to the marvelous hurdy-gurdy as possibly the greatest shot in his career. It shows Robert smiling in a mixture of pride and embarrassment as he introduces his technological pièce de résistance.

6

The Rules of the Game

Thus far I have been trying to develop two principal ideas: first, that despite the special character of film there is no unbridgeable chasm between it and the older representational arts; and second, that filmmaking requires a quasi-literary imagination in order to discover and create meanings that arise from more than mere reliance upon the visual. Panofsky enunciates something similar through his "principle of coexpressibility." But, as I will argue in the final pages of this book, Panofsky's attempt to harmonize the visual and the literary is undermined by his implied subordination of the latter to the former. Here I want to ask whether we even know what subordination means in this context. Obviously it entails some kind of sacrifice; but how or where or when should that occur?

This seems to me an area in which fixed rules cannot be set. Filmmakers will have to combine the two modes of imagination for themselves, in their own way, in accordance with their individual talents and inspiration. Harmonizing the visual and the literary, they may have to limit the former on some occasions instead of the latter. No theorist can lay down, as a general rule, more precise criteria than that.

It is only by trial and error, and by savoring creativity's sweet and bitter fruits that a cinematic artist can determine which mode of harmonization is worth repeating or developing further. The most we might ordain a priori is that the literary and the visual must both be subordinated to a perspective upon the world—a system of feelings and beliefs—that can be presented in a mixed medium such as film. This perspective need only be true to human nature, and vivid enough to reach an available audience.

Seen in this context, the greatness of Jean Renoir takes on new relevance. While *Death in Venice* falters because of the filmmaker's misplaced faith in the independent power of the visual to show forth interesting ideas by itself, *The Rules of the Game* endlessly fascinates because of the profound ambiguities that reverberate in its literary structure. These ambiguities occur within a flow of resonant and intelligible images whose content is always informed by conceptual ramifications that could never have come from sight alone. Renoir's film acquires philosophic scope—its penetration into reality at a significant level—by getting us to think about human relations in a way that is neither purely visual nor purely literary but instead an indissoluble coalescence of the two.

Discussing *Death in Venice*, I suggested that it could be experienced as an attempt to understand and express the idea of desire at a distance. To that extent, it investigates the nature of communication as well as the irremediable isolation that separates Aschenbach from Tadzio. *The Rules of the Game* also raises questions about the capacity of human beings to communicate their feelings, but in doing so it reveals that beneath this problem there lies one that is more elusive: the difficulty people have in trying to learn what their feelings really are.

Renoir's preoccupation with communication appears in the very first shots. As the film begins, we see a technician huddled over his switchboard equipment. Moving backward, the camera follows a radio cable unwinding from its source. The cable takes us to the radio announcer broadcasting from the airport tarmac where André will shortly land after his solo flight across the Atlantic. Through her ability to communicate at a distance via the microphone, the announcer gives André his opportunity to air his feelings about the woman he loves. He does that, but badly and in violation of the rules in his society. The tragi-comedy then unrolls in the narrative like the coil of the initiating cable.

A few shots later, we see the back of a radio set, and even the tubes that are emitting the message André has sent to the absent woman with whom he wants to communicate. She is listening to the blaring radio while finishing her toilette. Her name is Christine, and her husband Robert (the marquis) is then shown hearing the same transmission on a radio in another room. Elsewhere in Paris the guests of Geneviève, Robert's mistress, are also tuned in. Their comments about André's statement to the microphone reveal its

implications for the little world to which Christine and
Robert belong.

These characters will all come together at the chateau
in the country where most of the movie takes place.
There the radio is used as a link between the servants in
the kitchen and the masters upstairs. Though they also
communicate directly on many occasions, servants and
masters are joint recipients, in their separated domains,
of the same programs of broadcast music. Not only does
this enable Renoir to move seamlessly from one part of
the chateau into another but also his dissolves from
scene to scene are effected by means of an easily recognizable physical object that unifies the action. The radio
serves as a correlative for interpersonal communication,
which turns out to be chaotic and uncertain partly because of its dependence on mechanical technology.

More specifically, the radio is a metaphoric cognate
for the camera as it too communicates distant sights and
sounds. An actual camera is never shown within the
movie, but Renoir's fascination with this mainstay of his
medium appears in one remarkable scene. All of the
disorder that happens in the chateau starts after
Christine has seen her husband embracing Geneviève as
they stand in a remote stretch of open field. The hunt
has just ended and someone (Berthelin) gives Christine
a monocular field glass with which to study a squirrel
that runs along the branch of a tree. Extolling the virtues
of the instrument, Berthelin says: "It's optically so
refined, and it's so well put together that you can use it
as a magnifying glass at a short distance, and examine
this little squirrel without frightening it, and can live
every detail of its life with it."[1]

While this is being said, the camera shows us the squirrel that Christine is observing. A little later the camera captures the revelatory embrace between husband and mistress, and Christine sees that too through the field glass. But what is particularly interesting in the shots of both the squirrel and the embrace is the fact that they occur in close-ups that present them to us as they look to a camera zooming in, and not as they would be seen through a field glass. Berthelin's commentary thus applies to the optical potency of film—its ability to let us live every detail of Robert's life as well as Christine's awareness at a distance of his intimacy with another woman.

As mechanisms of communication, the radio, the field glass, and the camera can give us indirect knowledge about other people, but the technology cannot guarantee against errors of application to which men and women are prone. Though he is a perceptive person, Robert can never know with certainty whether he has interpreted Christine's subsequent attitude correctly, just as Christine has no way of knowing that Robert kisses Geneviève as part of a ritual of final separation. Having heard André's message to Christine over the radio, some of the guests assume that he and Christine are lovers in the sense that Robert and Geneviève have been. But that is not the case.

By the end of the film what has been shown is not the nature of love but rather the common failure to communicate it effectively, or even to know when it exists. In her effort to avenge herself on her husband, does Christine love any of the other men she encourages? Though she is concerned about her relationship with Robert and sadly tells her maid Lisette how much she yearns to have children, Christine sports with Saint-Aubin, then informs André that she does reciprocate his love, and a few minutes later assures her old friend Octave that in fact he is the one she has always loved.

The feelings of Octave and Robert are equally confused, and even André ends up as something less than the lover Christine thought he was. By invoking the rules of hospitality and refusing to steal Christine from her husband without having first notified him, he reveals to her that his is not the kind of love that he seemed to be professing. His declaration of honorable but unimpetuous devotion does not get through to her. In her state of agitation, she finds it insufficiently romantic. After André dies, Christine returns to the chateau as a chastened wife who must renew her struggle for marital communication while also feeling that her emotional turmoil was, in part, the cause of André's death.

As I have mentioned, Renoir studies the problems of affective communication by reference to his own creativity as a filmmaker. It is not coincidental that he plays the role of Octave. Being the grand mediator, Octave takes upon himself the attempt to bring his friends into harmonious relations with one another. He conveys André's fervent intentions to Christine, he advises Robert and Geneviève how to act, and in general he behaves as a directorial go-between and organizing intelligence within the group. But he is also a clumsy meddler whose bungling brings havoc upon his friends. At a crucial moment, he carries out romantic fantasies of his own even though he thereby betrays the trust of both Robert and André. He finally becomes an unwitting cog in the chain of events that leads to the shooting of André.

In Octave's mild annoyance at the fact that people oddly resist his desire to organize their lives, to fit them into affective roles that he can direct, one may see a wry comment by Renoir upon his own need to dominate the artists he has gathered for the sake of making a movie. "Everyone has his reasons," Octave complains, but Renoir can show what his are only by getting the others to perform the script he has written for them as well as for himself.

At the same time, we must remember that—unlike *8 1/2* and other films that deal with the dynamics of filmmaking—*The Rules of the Game* is not primarily about Renoir's situation as a director. Though Bazin is mistaken in thinking that Renoir stands at a distance from his subject matter and portrays it objectively without intruding his own personality, the outlook that Renoir does express in this film involves a segment of human life that far exceeds his own professional problems while also including them as well.

In interviews he gave after the film was made, Renoir remarks that the idea for this work came from dramas by Beaumarchais, Marivaux, and Musset. The film opens with a quote from *The Marriage of Figaro* by Beaumarchais together with a Mozart minuet that suggests much of the same spirit. The rapidity of the action and the liberal attitude toward sexual dalliance are reminiscent of Marivaux. But Musset's contribution is even more fundamental, in the sense in which an original text is basic to its adaptation, even though Renoir's movie transcends any source it may have had.

A preliminary title that Renoir considered for his film was *Les Caprices de Marianne,* and if one looks at the play by Musset with this title, one is struck by its similarities to *The Rules of the Game.* To begin with, both have a character named Octave who assumes the function of intermediary. He agrees to plead with Marianne on behalf of his friend, a pure-minded and idealistic person like André. That man's name is Coelio, signifying his place in the skies, just as André is a renowned aviator. Like André, Coelio is brought to earth, at first because of the lady's coldness, and eventually because he is killed by her husband's henchmen, just as André is shot by Robert's gamekeeper Schumacher. Marianne is married to the chief magistrate, whose station in society is parallel to the position of Robert the wealthy aristocrat. In both works Octave's involvement becomes ambiguous once he tries to communicate another's emotions. Marianne prefers him to Coelio, and it is only by a fortuitous switching of identities that Coelio is murdered instead of Octave.

With this as its origin in a Romantic tragi-comedy of the previous century, the film introduces dissimilarities that give it a unique splendor of its own. In Musset, Marianne's spouse is little more than the rigid, boorish, and ridiculous domestic tyrant that true lovers have always had to contend with. He is dangerous because of his jealousy and authoritarian madness, but he is hardly a personage who engages our attention otherwise.

Renoir's marquis, however, is one of the great characters of all dramatic art.

Though he belongs to what had become a very select society in 1939, the date of the story as well as the year the film was made, Robert is a delicate, sympathetic, and quite beguiling little man who finds it hard to give commands or assert his prerogatives. At the end he weeps because he feels unworthy of his triumph over André. In a joint interview with Marcel Dalio, who plays Robert, Renoir says that he wanted him for the role because he was "the only actor who could express a certain feeling of insecurity which is the basis of the character" (11). The effect was increased by having Dalio shave off his mustache. That made him look even less distinguished than usual. It also helped him bring out the comedic aspect of Robert's personality. At the height of his troubles, Robert exclaims: "I'm suffering. . . , and I have a *horror* of that!"—as if he thinks that only he might feel this way about suffering.

Dalio was a perfect choice for the role, which projects a series of ambiguities that this actor could convey just in walking across the room. When André arrives in the chateau, Robert strides quickly from one side of the entrance hall to the other, beaming as he welcomes him to his manor. Robert is the official host and proud possessor of all the audience surveys, including Christine, whom he stands beside with his arm around her shoulder as proof of their marital unity. But the movements of this twentieth-century marquis are so ungainly in their hasty excitement, and his good will is so obvious as he exudes his innocent pleasure in greeting a celebrity, that no one can think of him as even remotely autocratic. I choose this scene because it is suggestively conceived and beautifully enacted. From the beginning to the end of the film, Robert appears as an awkward and highly vulnerable person. Nothing of the sort exists in Musset.

The nineteenth-century play continues a long history of Western love literature that Renoir presupposes and freely blends with the domestic comedies that had been popular on the stage for many years. Within those traditions, *The Marriage of Figaro*, in the versions of both Beaumarchais and Mozart, has exceptional importance. In its own art form, each of them manifests a split that pervades the erotic consciousness of the modern world. It recurs in many films, and supremely in *The Rules of the Game*. Writing on sexual love, I have tried to characterize this split by distinguishing between "the sensuous" and "the passionate."[2] Musset's play is constructed precisely over the geologic fault that distinction seeks to explicate. Coelio is the embodiment of Romantic ideas about passion. He is hopelessly driven by the fervor of his affections, incapable of living without the beloved, and in fact suicidal when he suspects that she may prefer another man. For his part, Octave portrays himself as one who cares only about the pleasures of the senses—drinking, wenching, and enjoying each passing moment as it presents itself. Subsequent events disclose that there is much more to Octave; but the unmistakable difference between the two phenomenologies creates the dramatic tensions Musset exploits throughout his play.

In the case of Mozart, I argued that a lifelong concern along these lines manifests itself in much of his music and determines the expressive profundities in his greatest operas. In *Don Giovanni* the conflict between the sensuous and the passionate occurs with unswerving stridency, each being articulated with a kind of analytical detachment that results from Mozart's desire in that work to formulate the psychosexual problem instead of searching for an acceptable solution to it.

On the other hand, *The Marriage of Figaro* mainly explores divisions within the sensuous, possibly because of the influence of Beaumarchais's original. Rather than analyzing the two attitudes without taking sides in their struggle with each other, Mozart uses *The Marriage of Figaro* to concentrate on political maneuvering within the sensuous and apart from any passionate elements that also matter. Figaro and Susanna are not Romantic lovers who live or die for passion. They are in love, but their ardor is tempered by attachment to the hedonic possibilities of the sensuous. They see no reason why the count should have exclusive dominance in its domain, and that egalitarian feeling leads them to oppose him. They win out because of the strength of purpose that unites them in their search for sensuous goodness.[3]

I make these rudimentary comments about the Mozart operas because it seems to me essential to realize that *The Rules of the Game* devolves from *Don Giovanni* more than from *The Marriage of Figaro*. Like Musset before him, Renoir offers no comforting solutions in this film. His work is filled with ambiguities because it pits the different types of erotic sensibility against each other without offering any hope of harmonization between them. The passage from Beaumarchais that we see on the screen at the very beginning would lead us to expect a bedroom farce devoted to flighty vicissitudes of the sensuous. After the first title card announces that "this entertainment does not aspire to be a study of morals,"[4] we read the speech from Beaumarchais's *The Marriage of Figaro* that claims love must always be inconstant: "If love has wings, / Are they not to flutter?" As a matter of fact, however, the film deals less with the flutterings of love (even those of the aviator who flies through the air on wings) than with its inability to stay aloft in an atmosphere such as ours. In portraying this human predicament, and in making us wonder whether men and women can cope with it, the film is indeed a "study" of morals. It delineates the passionate and the sensuous in mortal combat that is dramatic as well as joyously comedic—*dramma giocosa*, as Mozart subtitles *Don Giovanni*.

In Renoir's film the passionate appears in the emotionality that André proclaims and that Schumacher turns into action as an expression of jealous love for his wife Lisette. Contrasting with the passionate, there is the sensuous playfulness that Octave, Lisette, and Marceau the poacher represent, that Christine tries to emulate, and that Geneviève considers distinctive of high society. Disappointed in her relations with Robert, Geneviève cites (but misquotes) the famous remark of Chamfort about love being the superficial contact of two epidermises—in other words, just a sensuous and emotionally insignificant encounter between bodily surfaces, not even persons.

By demonstrating that André's passion is dubious and possibly shallow, since he fails to run away with

Christine once she finally offers herself to him, and that Schumacher is criminally insane when he tries to execute Marceau and then blindly kills André, Renoir might seem to be siding with the sensuous. But that is not his intention, as it was also not Musset's. Even Octave, who believes in the sensuous, apologizes to Christine for André's unromantic reception of her responsive love. Octave says that André is living "the drama of all modern heroes. People like him, when they're in the air, they're great . . . and then when they touch down again, they're weak, they're pitiful, they're disarmed" (153–154). Given a chance to displace André, Octave is ready to throw himself into the dream of passionate love, as sensuous people dissatisfied with their love life often are. Only after Lisette chides Octave for being unrealistic about the kind of existence Christine would have does he see that it would be foolish for him to leave with her. The passionate is shown to be dangerous and precarious, but not necessary undesirable. Neither Musset nor Renoir wants to subjugate it for the sake of glorifying the sensuous.

In his analysis of comic structures in the movies, Gerald Mast misconstrues *The Rules of the Game* when he says: "Renoir's film is built on the proposition that good form is more important than sincere expression of feeling."[5] As I have been arguing, Renoir's conception is more highly nuanced than that would indicate.

The most consummate exponent of the sensuous is Marceau, who informs Robert that you can do anything you want with a woman if only you know how to make her laugh. But even Marceau is sympathetically moved when he sees that the loss of Lisette has devastated Schumacher and reduced him to tears. Moreover, there is the sense of authenticity and affective rightness that Robert feels when he realizes he has been fighting passionately, physically, tooth and nail like a common laborer, to hold on to the wife he now is willing to give up *because* he loves her so much.

In saying, however, that Renoir refuses to subordinate the passionate to the sensuous, I do not mean that he adheres to passion as a Romantic might. When André and Robert resort to fisticuffs, their fight over the woman they both wish to possess is strictly comical. Neither can throw a punch without making himself look ridiculous. We watch them with the same glee as when we observe the violence of clowns in the circus who strike each other in the face. Though we know that the behavior of Renoir's characters must be motivated by strong emotions, their uncoordinated movements are too outlandish for us to focus upon the feelings that are being expressed by them.

In a similar fashion, Renoir turns Schumacher's murderous search for Marceau into farcical entertainment—as the guests interpret it—so that our awareness that the gun is loaded with real bullets being fired by a man who is temporarily deranged by passion can hardly balance our unrestrained delight in seeing the small and likable Marceau elude his big and unrelenting pursuer.

At each point the sensuous reasserts itself (for love was made to flutter) but always in opposition to that passionate attitude that must nevertheless be respected within its limits. Geneviève begs Robert to give her one last ardent embrace on the occasion Christine observes with jealousy despite her calm demeanor. Passion is something Renoir takes seriously, while also reviling traditional attempts to make it paramount. His ambiguity in erotic matters remains as an incessant motor throughout this film.

The affective counterpoint I have been describing is but one of several ambiguities within *The Rules of the Game.* Whatever love may be, Renoir pits it against the ideal of friendship. In *Grand Illusion* he had already touched upon the dramatic differences between them. By the end of that film the oneness between the escapees (and between them and the aristocrat who risks his life for them) has been firmly established, whereas the permanence of Maréchal's love for the German woman is unproved and possibly an illusion. In an earlier version of the script the escapees agree to meet at Maxim's, the fashionable Parisian restaurant, after the war is over; but neither of them shows up. This questioning of friendship as a human reality is excluded in the more affirmative conclusion that Renoir finally chose for that film.

Throughout *The Rules of the Game,* made the following year, he continues the analyses of friendship and love, and their relation to each other. André flies the Atlantic as an absurdist act that has meaning for him only because he did it for the woman he loves—a motif reminiscent of the exploits of courtly lovers in the Middle Ages. Yet the one who embraces him at the airport is his buddy Octave, whose bear hug is an

expression of his warm but possibly smothering friendship for André. Robert shrewdly calls Octave "a dangerous poet," and in fact Octave extends toward all his
friends an infectious conviviality and imaginative good
will while also embroiling them in schemes of his own
choosing that end badly for them.

When Octave masquerades at the evening entertainment in the skin of an actual bear, we see how clumsy
he can be. Is his failure to manage his friends' affairs a
moral deficiency in him, or in the culture that he
typifies? Octave offers both as likely explanations. He
tells Christine that his life has come to naught, and later
he identifies with Marceau as an outsider who has been
poaching on the benevolence of others without providing them the human services they have a right to expect
in return.

Indeed we have seen Octave in the early scenes move
back and forth between the incompatible desires of
André and Robert, helping the former in his attempt to
get Christine and suggesting to the latter that he dispose
of Geneviève by pushing her toward André. In all this,
Octave seems to have no conception of his own duplicity.
With his bearlike bluster he seems merely humorous,
wheedling first Christine and then Robert to invite
André to their country estate. He does not have Robert's
interests at heart; and even Christine wonders about his
friendship for her once she realizes that he has known,
but not told her, that Geneviève is Robert's mistress.

Octave defends himself by saying that nowadays, in
society at large, everyone lies. In other words, the
authentic communication toward which true friendship

aspires is no longer possible in the present state of civilization. After André is killed, Octave departs as soon as he can. He sees that he has betrayed these people, and he knows that for him life in their world is now unthinkable. There will be official inquiries at which he would be expected to lie about the circumstances of André's death, as Robert automatically does in calling it an accident. This enlarged network of deception is more than Octave can face.

But the fact remains that, at the moment of truth, Octave does live up to the one great friendship that has provided a meaningful mission for him from the very outset. Giving André the overcoat he himself has been wearing, thus enclosing him in a final bear hug, Octave renounces his own feelings about Christine as an act of supervening friendship toward André.

One could also say that Octave, like Robert, loves Christine enough to step aside and let her go with the man who can best make her happy. By this time in the film, however, the ideal of love has been so vastly tarnished that we interpret Octave's sacrificial decision as an expression of friendship, toward Christine as well as André, rather than as love for her. There is no reason to say, as at least one critic has, that Octave sends his best friend to his death. Despite his weakness and fallibility, Octave is still devoted to the man—the only person in this film who knows how to fly—for whom he obviously has a kind of hero worship.

In Musset the ideal of male friendship resounds defiantly at the tragic finale. Octave there rejects Marianne's declaration of love because he refuses to dishonor himself by profiting from his friend's disaster. Coelio having been murdered, there is nothing Marianne can provide that would exorcise Octave's grief for the friendship he has lost forever.

In *The Rules of the Game* the conflict between love and friendship perturbs the women as much as the men. Towards the beginning we learn that Christine had wanted from André nothing but friendship, only to have awakened in him a love that she did not foresee. To eliminate any suspicion of scandal, she proclaims to the guests that her relationship with André is and was based only on the purest friendship. Earlier, when she asks Lisette about the latter's love affairs, the two women discuss the possibility of being friends with a man. Lisette thinks it is as rare as seeing the moon in broad daylight, preparing us for the moonlit scenes at the end of the film in which Christine's experiments with love and friendship run their course.

Like Susanna in *The Marriage of Figaro*, Zerlina in *Don Giovanni*, and with some modifications Despina in *Così fan tutte*, Lisette finds it hard to believe that men and women can ever be friends with one another. Her sensuous disposition is itself a kind of friendly playfulness that easily becomes erotic sport, as also happens to her counterparts in the Mozart operas. But that is not the kind of love that Christine has in mind. Not being a sensuous woman herself, she fails to understand that her gallant conversations with André, or her frolicking with Octave on her bed, may not be considered mere friendliness, as she naively assumes. After her harrowing experience later on, she has learned a lesson.

For his part, Robert the gentle aristocrat embodies the goodness of both friendliness and friendship throughout the film. Ludicrous as he often seems, he nevertheless captures our respect for the compassion with which he tries to separate himself from a mistress he no longer loves, the politeness he constantly accords his wife, the warmth (and money) he offers an old crony like Octave, the humanitarian spirit he unaffectedly displays in his relations with Marceau, Schumacher, and the other servants. At the very moment that Octave and Christine are making plans to walk out on him, Robert enunciates the abused ideal that will shortly resonate in Octave as well: "I don't believe in very much, you know," Robert says to André after their fight, "but it seems to me that I'm going to begin to believe in friendship" (160).

So powerful is this positive virtue that it brings together not only Robert and André but also Schumacher and Marceau. In each case, what eventuates is a friendship of mutual misery produced by love for women who are either fragile or frivolous. Whether or not the women are worth loving, they represent affective possibilities the men are able to approximate only by transmuting their joint self-pity into unforeseen male bonding.

Christine achieves something similar in her relationship with Geneviève. Once she tricks her into admitting that Robert is her lover, Christine has no difficulty singing and dancing with this rival female. But these two are not likely to become close to each other. Only in Lisette's loyalty to her mistress do we see among the women in this movie an intimation of the oneness that the principal males attain as a by-product of their

hapless search for love. In this emphasis upon the re-
deeming attributes of masculine friendship, *The Rules of
the Game* repeats the same conclusion, though at a much
deeper level of analysis, as the one that Renoir used for
Grand Illusion.

Where friends come together and communicate enjoy-
ably, one has a model of the good life. *The Rules of the
Game* has been interpreted as a critique of French society
of the thirties, and in one place Renoir says it shows "a
society in process of disintegration."[6] But his film can
also be interpreted as celebrating what was best in that
society. Renoir is not necessarily disingenuous when he
remarks, almost thirty years after the movie was made:
"People thought that, in writing *The Rules of the Game*, I
was criticizing society, but not at all. I wish I could live
in such a society—that would be wonderful" (13). He
then goes on to say that the society he depicted was not
"pure," that only André the heroic aviator was, and that
the narrative was just a projection of Renoir's own preoccupation with the problem of meeting people, entering
their company from the outside and learning how to
belong.

   The notion of purity, which we may also interpret as
a kind of idealistic simplemindedness, already occurred
in Musset's play. But the outsider's desire to be admitted
into a select society is something that comes from
Renoir's personal experience. Though Musset's Coelio
and Octave are indeed outsiders, neither pays much
attention to this fact about themselves. The film's André

and Octave—to say nothing of Marceau the little poacher and his oppressor Schumacher—are always aware that they are intruders upon a social world that may at any moment withhold its life-sustaining goodness.

Perhaps Renoir considers André pure because he scorns the socialites who lionize him for having made his solo flight across the Atlantic. Yet he also accepts their way of life in order to accomplish the erotic pursuit that drives him on. All the other characters would seem to agree with Renoir about how wonderful it is to live in a world of such apparent gaiety and sophistication. Marceau wants nothing more than to be a domestic in the chateau. Octave obviously relishes his role as court jester. The guests move about as if the universe had nothing better to do than to satisfy their momentary whims.

As an accomplice in this attitude toward life, Renoir's camera lovingly portrays the sumptuous apartments in Paris, the great estate in the country, and all the other appurtenances of accumulated wealth. Through close-up and deep-focus shots, it savors their sweet and seductive charm. Even the mechanized reminders of the eighteenth century, the wound-up dolls and warblers, accentuate the glamorous image of aristocratic *douceur de vivre*.

From this point of view, there is nothing revolutionary about *The Rules of the Game,* and one can see why Renoir was so surprised to discover that audiences in 1939 found the film subversive. "I was sure the public would like it—it was a light picture, parties are not big problems, and the big problems were so well hidden that the audience wouldn't be hurt in their feelings. Well, I was very wrong" (13). What Renoir had not realized, and what makes his film so upsetting, is the fact that humankind cannot stand too much moral ambiguity. If the society he depicts is indeed so wonderful, why is it that only the supernumeraries are really at ease in it?

Even Robert and Christine are not. In a sense they too are outsiders. Though he is a marquis, and an "homme du monde" (as his chef says as a testament to his good taste in potato salads), Robert is partly Jewish in a society where his own servants are not afraid to voice their generic anti-Semitism. Dalio, whose real name was Israel Moshe Blauschild, looked Jewish to his French audience. The "insecurity" he introduced into his characterization shows forth as a discomfort he might well have felt as the ruler of this Proustian little clan.

For her part, Christine is a foreigner speaking French with a German accent. She is the daughter of an Austrian musician—himself a pinnacle of society, since he was a famous conductor—but she is scarcely comfortable in her adopted milieu. Mast says it is unlikely that men could fall in love with Nora Grégor, the actress who plays Christine, and he wonders what the film would have been like if Renoir had succeeded in getting the prettier Simone Simon for this role. But the fact that Christine does not look secure or delectable is just the point. Though her social status is high enough to elicit the interest of the appropriate males, her awkward movements (and even the ugly expanse of her back, which Renoir's camera exposes with a kind of clinical cruelty) bespeak her homelessness in this discriminating but somewhat vapid environment.

Though Renoir may have wanted to live as his characters do, he portrays their society as an artificial world that provides everything we need to enjoy life except for the ability itself. One thinks of the countess in Mozart's *Marriage of Figaro*, and of how much that opera would have lost if she had been presented as a woman who was fully sexual rather than repressed and emotionally vulnerable beneath her veneer of upper-class stolidity. If that is what Renoir had in mind, Nora Grégor was just right for the part.

Given Renoir's ambivalent perspective, one often senses personal problems that he may have felt within himself. Much of the film's spontaneity comes from the way he habitually did his work—his writing a preliminary script, his altering it in association with the actors, his treating the entire company as members of a creative society that exists for the sake of their communal art. An idealized version of this is articulated in the narrative of Renoir's earlier film *The Crime of M. Lange.* In his frequent use of tracking shots throughout *The Rules of the Game,* Renoir seems to be hovering over and around the action in which he also participates, since he too is one of the players.

Though it would be a fallacy to identify Octave with Renoir, one could extend what I was saying before about Renoir's partial identification with that character. Aside from his not belonging to the moneyed class on which he depends, Octave feels that his life is wasted because he has never found an audience for his talents. He spits into the moat outside the chateau like the feckless and parasitic courtiers who do the same or similar in Molière, and when he acts out his fantasy of conducting an orchestra, like Christine's father, he remarks that what has eluded him all along is "contact with the public."

One might think that Renoir himself had had no lack of such contact, since movies are able to reach a large number of people. Indeed *Grand Illusion* had just been a great success. All the same, a filmmaker is systematically hidden by his medium in a way that does not apply to an orchestra conductor. Like other musicians on stage, conductors perform in front of an immediate audience. Their aesthetic activity exists in the presence of men and women who have gathered to see and hear them as the human instantiations of music. In a film, as I have been suggesting, the director and his actors communicate through the very technology that alienates them and precludes the kind of rapport Octave longs to have. It is as if Renoir feared that his identity, which is to say his creative spirit, was only derivative from what appears in machine-made photographic images, instead of vice versa.

This may also underlie the use of theatrical performances in several of Renoir's films. Particularly when they occur in the midst of a party, as in *The Rules of the Game*, these amateur productions—which they sometimes are—throw people together in an aesthetic enactment of sheer gregariousness. In his *Letter to D'Alembert*, Rousseau attacked the institution of professional theater as an artificial inducement that keeps the audience passive and prevents it from acting out its feelings. As a substitute he recommended impromptu plays or festivities that enable everyone to take part in a communal and truly affective happening. To a limited extent, that is what Renoir shows us in each of these movies. We who watch the films can also join in, but only indirectly and at a distance. We are just spectators, and our participation must remain vicarious.

Renoir had reason to feel uncomfortable with the imperfection of this one-way communication required by his medium. His previous work was sometimes subjected to gross misinterpretation, which finally kept *The Rules of the Game* from reaching its proper audience for many years, and he had often suffered from monetary and irrelevant obstacles that restrained his attempt to make contact with a large public.

As a conductor manqué, Octave reminds us that music is an art arising from the harmony of different instruments, including the human voice. Having failed in his desire to orchestrate the feelings and behavior of his friends, Octave now understands that more is involved than the fact that everyone has his or her reasons, not all of which are even spoken. The narrative proves to him that he cannot conduct this small society of friends any more than he could lead an orchestra.

Despite his own success as an organizer of men and women, Renoir may have felt inadequate when compared with that other father figure who was renowned for his artistic and basically interpersonal achievement—Pierre Auguste Renoir, his biological father. The elder Renoir explained the evocative character of his works by saying he painted with his penis. It is something else to grapple with the urgencies of movie business and technology while exposing oneself in a medium that demands so many different kinds of skill.

At the same time, Renoir's attachment to his father was beneficial throughout his career, as evidenced in the book he wrote about their life together.[7] When Octave has his intimate conversation with Christine in her bedroom, we notice a small sculpture that is probably the bust Pierre Auguste made of Jean's brother Coco. As if acknowledging how much his father's art sustains and lives on in him, Renoir leans idly on the statuette. It remains as a silent presence in the drama of that scene.[8]

Renoir's participation in socialist and communist politics of the 1930s might well have made him that much more conscious of barriers to communication with the masses in a "light picture" such as *The Rules of the Game*. Perhaps because he was so ambivalent about the bourgeois society in which he lived without feeling he had a place in it, Renoir frequently contrasts that society with life in nature. Many commentators have noted that opposition between nature and social order as a whole is one of the major themes in virtually all his movies. *The Rules of the Game*, Renoir's most analytical film, starts in nature—the night sky from which André emerges—but quickly turns to human society in the form of crowds at Orly that greet the descended hero. Through the radio broadcast, they are linked to the Paris apartments of people who then revisit nature in the woods of Sologne. Sartre said that death is the final return to nature, and that happens to André.

The city folk would all seem to be traveling in search of the benign nature from which André originated. They find it in other films of Renoir, but not in this one. In *The Rules* the countryside is dominated by the social hegemony of the chateau. Even the animals run on command, as in the hunt where an army of beaters regiments their move across the field of fire. Schumacher's reverential words about the primitive life of unspoiled nature as it exists in Alsace are repeated by Lisette, but only as a way of humoring him while Marceau sneaks through the kitchen. As he learns to his sorrow, Schumacher cannot get his wife to stay with him either in Sologne or Alsace, since she likes being a servant and prefers the artificial pleasures of Parisian urban life.

In portraying an attempted voyage from society into nature, Renoir plays a variation upon a familiar theme in Western drama. One need only think of *As You Like It* or *A Midsummer Night's Dream* (which Renoir's film resembles in also having a performance within the play and a masquerading of identities). While renewing this literary tradition, Renoir's perspective is always cinematic and distinctly contemporary. Being a man of the twentieth century, he shows how easily the destruction of nature can lead to the destruction of civilized society. Before the hunt Saint-Aubin and La Bruyère resolve the question of a disputed pheasant in the most polite and cordial manner one could imagine; after having killed birds and beasts in their ceremonial massacre, they seem ready to murder each other as the means of settling who rightly owns one of the slaughtered creatures. Taking another step in the same direction, we sense Renoir's anxiety about the coming war that used nature as a battleground and endangered humanity indiscriminately.

Like his other films that portray civilization's suicidal assault upon nature, this one reveals how people can be deprived of what is innately natural in themselves.

Though Schumacher's sexual passion causes him to fire at André, we know that André has already been denatured as a lover. He suppresses his amatory drive in acceding to the restrictions of society. If one cannot live with the woman one loves because of the conventions to which André alludes, one is throttling sexual impulse for the sake of an invasive code of civilization. Renoir views the struggle between them much as Freud did in *Civilization and Its Discontents*, and he, too, despairs of any happy solution.

At least, within the film itself Renoir suggests no way out. The greatness of *The Rules of the Game* issues from his cinematic fertility in creating correlative objects, and correlative occurrences, that are visually meaningful while being able to disclose affective problems in human relations. One of the correlative objects is the vase of gladioli that fascinate Robert at the end of the scene in Geneviève's apartment. He has been trying to divest himself of his mistress without hurting her feelings or falsifying his own. Neither can handle the situation, and Renoir highlights how difficult it is by having the camera balance their human frailty against the self-assured serenity of the Buddhas that stand on pedestals next to them in the apartment. After he has yielded to Geneviève's entreaties and revoked his decision to terminate their liaison, Robert nervously prunes the gladioli. It is what ethologists call displacement behavior, his venting his frustration by picking at these helpless but convenient objects. In throwing away defects in the flowers, however, he is testifying to his inability to fit nature into a civilized design of his choosing. He cannot be cruel to Geneviève because that would violate his own nature, which is inoffensive, and also constitute a lack of civility.

Robert is motivated by a similar concern when he later informs Schumacher that he wants to get rid of the rabbits without putting up fences. He had previously told Octave how much he hates barriers, which is why he invites André to the country estate. If everything comes out in the open, society may be able to regulate unruly passions. That, at least, is what he hopes will happen. The subsequent events prove him to have been overly optimistic. Nature and society are not easily reconciled. People are liable to destruction just as rabbits are.

The greenhouse outside the chateau also serves as a correlative object, and so does Octave's hat. Troubled by her discovery that André lacks the natural force she had expected in a lover, Christine leads Octave into the night air. She will not return to the chateau, that is, society, but neither does she want to wander through the woods on this chilly evening. They end up in the greenhouse, which functions as a symbol of possible harmony between nature and civilization. It is there that she and Octave reach their feverish decision about a course of action. The greenhouse eventually becomes the unattained goal of André's last solo.

Before that can happen, Octave must return to the chateau, where he encounters Lisette and her civilized scruples about Christine's need for social benefits that life with Octave would not allow. Octave pretends not to hear her, feigning anxiety about his lost hat. But once he locates this symbol of customary attire and protection against the elements of nature, he acts like one who has found his head and can now think clearly. When Lisette berates Octave, he glances at a mirror behind them. He sees not himself or an imaginary image of what he is, but only ocular proof that the world will agree with Lisette in thinking him too old for Christine. He withdraws in favor of André, who is younger than he. Civilization thus wins out, though nature takes its revenge by bringing down the hero.

Marceau, who knows about the killing of animals, is the one who says that André fell to his death "comme une bête." André dies as the sacrificial lamb who represented, but could not perpetuate, the most elevated ideals of his society. Like spirit itself, they too are products of nature, and in many ways as subservient to it as all the rest of animality. Berthelin's field glass reveals that human beings embracing in what looks like an expression of love are not very different from a squirrel scampering on the branch of a tree.

Having remembered that scene, and what followed from it, we are forced to reconsider the symbolism of the greenhouse. Far from being a satisfying destination, it now appears as just another locale for the arrangement of imperfect flowers like the ones in Geneviève's apartment. In both settings the attempt to civilize nature culminates in futility. After André's death, Christine staunchly marches back to the chateau, renews her marital relations with Robert, and undoubtedly discovers that he is no longer bound to his mistress. Since that separation was already in progress at the beginning of the film, nothing much has been achieved. But perhaps Christine, who encourages her niece Jackie to make a brave show in public, will now accept the fact that her personal nature cannot be fulfilled apart from this society.

In the meantime, Octave, the dangerous poet, has been removed from the floral display that is the civilized world he was disturbing while trying to rearrange it by himself. With André and Geneviève out of the way, order has been restored through a victory of social conformity. The same occurs at Lisette's level in the elimination of both Schumacher and Marceau. The estate has been freed of poachers as well as unwanted rabbits, but the somber climax reminds us that nature always has the last word. It asserts itself in the sheer finality of death.

In the party scene, that was the meaning of the dance of skeletons and the spooky playing of Saint-Saëns's *danse macabre* on the player piano. It operates mechanically, beyond human control, like death itself. Charlotte, the pianist among the guests who has now been superseded by the robotic action of the keys, regards their movement with an appropriate look of awe and trepidation. Something similar applies to Robert's hurdy-gurdy, the music machine whose sudden breakdown is correlated with the collapse of civilized behavior when Schumacher chases Marceau with intent to kill. Technology then appears as a secret agent of the destructive element in nature. In the last moments of the film, miniature cypress trees stand in a regular order before the chateau. Their little wooden tubs contain nature within another floral pattern that society has neatly ordained. The cypress tree is, however, an ancient and frequent symbol of death. Renoir's camera lingers over this paradox, giving us ample time to digest its grave ambiguity.

Much of what I have been saying about *The Rules of the Game* can be reformulated in terms of an antithesis, between the human and the technical, that amplifies my comments about film as both communication and alienation. To say that technology is a problem for modern man is to say what people even in 1939 could perceive as a truism about our present moral condition. Renoir's brilliance consists in posing the issue imaginatively throughout his fiction while suggesting that many of the good things in life—games of love and chance, mechanical toys, and that cinematic art we enjoy so much—are at the same time both natural and artificial, meaningful in terms of instinctual nature as well as contrived techniques.

Renoir hints that the same may be true of people themselves. We are also machines, albeit conscious ones, that can break at any time. Geneviève having her hysterical fit and Jackie fainting away malfunction like bits of machinery under strain. Corneille, the chateau's majordomo whose magisterial name fits his august demeanor, informs Robert that during Schumacher's shooting spree few of the gadgets have been broken and that all the guests are "*indemnes*" (undamaged), as if they too are just artifacts, fragile products of some technological and even mechanized manufacture.

The notion of play as organized pleasure permeates *The Rules of the Game*. The pillow-throwing, mock fencing, card games, and the hunt itself are examples of spontaneous but rule-regulated behavior as it interpenetrates the human values of friendship, love, and social feeling. Similarly, the dolls, the stuffed birds, and all the other finely crafted objects that we see remind us that life in society depends on orderliness, premeditation, and technical precision. In this comic tragedy whose story has nothing to do with the making of movies, we are never allowed to forget that Renoir's own medium is based on an automatic mechanism that transforms reality for the sake of the aesthetic qualities we care about as human beings.

Within the dialectical poles that Renoir presupposes, there resides a differentiation among various types of rules. In an early draft of his script, he describes his Christine character as believing that the socially approved rules of the marriage game require a woman to put up with an odious husband for the sake of having access to lovers she may prefer.[9] In the final version this cynical notion has been pared away and replaced by the analyses I have been discussing. The rules of society are presented as contrasting with the rules of love. When André tells Christine that he must not abscond with her without informing Robert, he negates the rules of passionate love as formulated by typical romanticism of the previous century. But he acts in accordance with longer lasting rules of morality. One does not steal the wife of one's host any more than one steals the silverware. It is because André has this well-mannered recognition of the rules for accepting hospitality that he and Robert can eventually become friends. But the reigning rules of love, at least when it appears as uncontrolled passion, cut across such proprieties.

Nor does social and legitimate restraint hold sway within the sensuous when it is detached from the rest of life, for example in the animal playfulness between Lisette and Marceau. Renoir repeatedly shows us cunning dolls that seem sexually inviting, and Lisette eats an apple on two occasions, like a preprogrammed Eve, as if her sensuous inclinations follow mechanical rules of their own. Going berserk in conformance with the rules of passion, Schumacher violates the rules of the sensuous in addition to those of society. The sensuous tells us to stay cool, to play but do no harm, to realize that the contact between two epidermises is mainly a matter of technique and does not mean very much.

One could argue that Robert, as the quasi-magistrate who administers the different rules in his society, is responsible for the painful chaos that erupts. If he had been sufficiently dedicated to the civilized conventions, he would have excluded André in advance, invoking the rules of marriage as a reason for keeping him away from Christine. He does not behave that way, just as he does not prosecute Marceau for poaching rabbits. Hating barriers, as he would, being partly an outsider himself, Robert has brought the interlopers into society. Renoir refers to Dalio standing next to the marvelous hurdy-gurdy as possibly the greatest shot in his career. It shows Robert smiling in a mixture of pride and embarrassment as he introduces his technological *pièce de résistance.*

When it breaks down, shortly afterwards, it symbolizes the catastrophic consequences that come from Robert's mismanagement of the rules that prevail in modern life.

These rules interact in ways that neither Robert nor Octave, nor anyone else perhaps, can control as they thought they might. In affective reality disorder is contagious. Though stability is restored once the disturbing elements have been exorcised, we are shaken in our confidence that human beings can master the machinery of their social being. The tears in Robert's eyes when he tells the guests that André has died express his sense of inadequacy. And with him, everyone has failed. He weeps for us as well as for himself.

Throughout all this, however, Renoir's art has been transforming these failures in keeping with *its* rules. Therein lies the ultimate hope of humanity. More than almost any other filmmaker, Renoir has taught us how to proceed.[10]

Conclusion: Cinematic Transformation

I have been studying the human import of cinematic art, treating it as a vehicle for expressing ideas as well as feelings. Formalist aesthetics concerns itself with the *means* by which film attains this cognitive and affective capacity. The formalist approach can readily cooperate with attempts to elucidate what is meaningful in particular works of cinema, and at its best it reveals how meaning is conveyed through the technical procedures characteristic of film. But all too often, the formalist is so preoccupied with questions of technique that he or she neglects every other consideration and makes us wonder why this art form has mattered so much to so many people.

At this point one might explore the differences between art and craft or, from another direction, between art and mere entertainment. When cinema first began, many people doubted that it could ever be anything other than mindless pleasure for the eyes. That question has long since been settled, however, and in our age we do better to delineate the varied ways that film can excel as both an art form and a source of immediate enjoyment.

In that seminal article to which I referred, Panofsky formulates what he calls "the principle of coexpressibility" in an effort to understand the relationship between different components within a film. Panofsky addresses himself to the possible cooperation between words and images. What we hear in a film, he says, "remains, for good or worse, inextricably fused with that which we see; the sound, articulate or not, cannot express any more than is expressed, at the same time, by visible movement; and in a good film it does not even attempt to do so."[1] On the face of it, this principle would seem to be indubitable. The dialogue (and the scenario as a whole) cannot be completely separated from the visible action that we watch on screen. The two serve as interrelated elements that may or may not be "fused" but that must certainly be integrated with each other.

When we read Panofsky a second time, however, we perceive that he is advocating a kind of puristic approach to the visual. What does it mean to say that sound cannot express any more than is expressed by visible movement? If there is indeed a harmonious merging of words and images, should we not conclude that neither can express more than the other? It seems clear that Panofsky is arguing for a special type of coexpressibility, one in which sound is inherently subordinate to sight. And in fact he condemns the use of dialogue that is too "poetic," on the grounds that this weakens the rightful dominance of visual expressiveness.

In Panofsky's defense, one might cite film adaptations that greatly revise their literary sources and yet succeed within their own medium. Two Shakespearean examples will be enough to make the point. Max Reinhardt's *A Midsummer Night's Dream* is little short of a desecration of its original, Shakespeare's poetry having been torn to shreds and often excised ruthlessly. But in the process, the film attains an aery lightness through its visual presentation that no faithful rendering of the spoken text could have approximated. In Olivier's *Henry V,* liberties are taken with the background for scenes in France. As a contrast to the realistic portrayal he needed for most of the film, Olivier wanted to draw upon the pictorial effects of the medieval miniature paintings known as *Les Très Riches Heures du Duc de Berri*.[2] In an interview, Olivier remarks that he also hoped the unreality of these and other sets would cause more literal-minded people in the audience to accept the fact that the characters, speaking Shakespeare's verse, were "talking so funny."[3]

The achievement of these two films, quite considerable in the case of Olivier's, could be used to support Panofsky's principle of coexpressibility. His idea has indeed been seconded by many theorists, and it does reflect the undeniable truth that great silent movies have existed, whereas a sound track by itself is not a film at all. But as often happens in aesthetics, extreme differences of this sort have little to do with the really interesting questions about the nature of an art form. We want to know not whether a picture is worth a thousand words, or a hundred, or ten, but whether the sensibility that belongs to literary imagination has substantial validity in cinematic art. I have the impression that Panofsky, like others who approach film from the point of view of their expertise in painting or still photography, tends to believe that the verbal is a minor, or at least a lesser, component of the medium.

But even in silent films the dialogue was extremely prominent. It is just that we could not hear it. We had to read an extract after having employed our imagination to decipher what was being uttered by human beings who were visible but not audible. Watching a silent movie is like being a deaf man observing the behavior of persons who are conversing with each other while also wanting to be understood by him.

That is why the gestures and movements of characters in silent films, especially the early ones, are so strenuously magnified. Before talkies were invented, these magnifications probably seemed less grotesque than they do to us, now that we have lost the habit of adjusting to them. Silent films required audiences to decode the visual scene without the aid of aural cues on which we usually rely, and without the advantage that lipreading provides to ordinary deaf people.

The purpose of this decoding process was to comprehend, of course, what was going on in the dramatic situation being enacted. But understanding of this sort could be achieved only by determining, as a problem in inductive logic, what the characters might be saying to each other. Far from being absent or irrelevant, the dialogue had enormous, though abnormal, import for the viewers' imagination.

In many ways this circumstance illustrates the similarity between film and opera. The relationship between sound and image in talking pictures is comparable to the relationship between words and music in operatic performances. In opposition to purists who claim that opera is aesthetic only through its music, I have elsewhere suggested that one should take the mixed character of this art at its face value, subordinating both words and music to the dramatic totality they normally subserve, and interpreting that in terms of its expressive capability.[4]

Since their inception, films have played a role in Western civilization parallel to the one that opera had in the nineteenth century. The contemporary decline of opera is related to the almost synchronized growth of cinematic art in popular culture. Both opera and film have the ability to draw upon affective levels of our being that no other arts can reach. Both are quasi-theatrical media that emancipated themselves from the current limitations of the stage. To appreciate the aesthetic potency of either film or opera, we must start with a principle of coexpressibility without any prior assumptions about how the different elements must be joined. The correct mode of unification depends on the individual artist and what he or she wishes to express. That will vary from work to work.

Since I know my suggestion will be a puzzlement for many people who respond to the visual grandeur of even inferior films, let me clarify it a little further. In cinema we have a mixed medium that includes words, images, and often music, some of it even operatic music. But just as one could argue that music is subordinate to the rest of film, and sometimes eliminated entirely, so too does the purist want to subordinate sound to sight.

In rejecting any rigid hierarchy, I am not denying that the visual component yields a kind of meaning that sound alone can never have. Nor do I believe that a screenplay should be readable as poetry or drama or some type of shorthand novel. Since the camera is an eye that serves the mind of an artist who has learned to observe cinematically, it sees whatever it surveys with an intelligence that only a person who knows *how to look* can bring to bear. The visual then operates through a system of meanings, however inchoate and untranslatable they may be, that fructify but are not reducible to verbal types of communication.

To this extent, film is an exemplar of human reality in general. The world we live in, the visible world that we encounter as persons interacting with one another and with the natural environment that both sustains and threatens us, is a world in which words and images unite throughout all their modes of signification. Assuming they have a language and are not impaired, people who see the picture of a table will recognize it as what the word *table* refers to. They cannot apprehend the meanings in the picture without drawing upon connotations that derive from a lifetime of using terms such as that one. And though language may often function without employing overtly imagistic effects, visual experience contributes—directly or indirectly—to all linguistic utterances other than the most abstract. It is not surprising, therefore, that language has its intimate and reciprocal relation to the visual.

This interpenetration binding word and image manifests the tie between concept and percept that I discussed earlier. I have always been struck by the oddness in Sartre's remark that once we name something, or describe it, we have already changed it. That seems so obviously true, and yet it is false to our actual experience. Walking through the woods in the fall, we may give ourselves to the total splendor of the visual panorama. We see an expanse of trees, fallen leaves, sky, sloping earth; we wallow in the chromatic brightness of the scene before us. If we depict it in words or deliberate about its contents, our experience does differ in some manner. The trees become birches, or beeches, or pines, or oaks; the brownish leaves lying on the ground become harbingers of proximate winter; and so on. It is as if our perceptual awareness has been displaced by conceptual interpretations that exceed what was immediately present in consciousness.

But this account is incomplete, and phenomenologically inaccurate. Naming or categorizing something does not alter our perception of reality, at least not necessarily. On the contrary, the conceptual may reinforce our percepts. We see what we saw before except that our ideation evokes further and richer ways of seeing. Nothing need be lost: where previously we noticed only trees, we now discern the different species among them; where we basked in the autumnal goodness of the turning colors, we now relish the great variety of their hues. The conceptual gives extra meaning to our visual encounter. It supplements the perceptual properties that were there before without supplanting them.

The error in Sartre's view comes from his apparent belief that language is an imposition upon some prior and more fundamental acquaintance with reality, as if words were a filter that stands between us and the world. The truth is that what we nominate as "the world" is itself an interwoven texture of concepts, linguistic either actually or potentially, as well as percepts. Different moments of consciousness involve different relations between percepts and concepts. Nothing perceptual occurs without conceptual implications of some sort. However visual an art may be, its aesthetic quality derives from a network of meanings that are conceptual and perceptual at the same time. Instead of separating concept and percept, film theory should be mapping out the diversities within structures of what can alternately be called conceptual perception or perceptual conception.

As we move toward that goal, we recognize increasingly that the glory of cinematic art emanates not from recording, duplicating, or literally capturing anything, but rather from creating meanings that transform our reality through conceptualized percepts and perceptualized concepts arising out of the techniques that film possesses. Relying on words (and music) in conjunction with its photographic images, film attends to some aspect of the world that a filmmaker selects for his or her communication. Artistic form is thereby produced, and that delights us as a consummatory value.

Everything in life is available for this, including non-verbal behavior. In a work of literature it would have to be described; in a film it can be shown in all its demonstrational beauty, as a Chaplin or a Keaton does. In themselves, as purely and wholly autonomous data of perception, the activities or events have no meaning. They become meaningful only as they enter into the life of people dynamically related to one another through words no less than visual gestures. Like the other arts, cinema draws upon our total participation in nature, the cognitive, affective, and sensory dimensions of our existence making a continuum of ends and means among themselves. The aesthetic transformations that result are consummations attuned to what we need and desire as creatures of our natural habitat.

That's entertainment, and also the basis of magnificent art. Critics can approach it from the vantage point of either realist or formalist types of intuition, and possibly by using both simultaneously. Far from being incompatible, these methodologies presuppose each other. However much a film may devote itself to visual reality, or any other, it can portray the world only through the artificial devices cultivated in the history of this medium. Its meaningfulness depends on that necessity.

By analyzing how transformations of the real come into being through perceptual presentations, the formalists augment our experience and our understanding. The realists do so by showing how film puts us in touch with what we are as human beings. Since the truth and meaning that formalists seek cannot be found without this additional approach, we need to develop a pluralistic and humanistic realism that works in tandem with whatever formalism is helpful at the moment. The future will belong to those who are able to effect this harmonization.

Notes

Introduction: Realism vs. Formalism

1. For a survey of classical realist and formalist theories, see J. Dudley Andrew, *The Major Film Theories: An Introduction* (New York: Oxford University Press, 1976). For selections from the relevant writings, see *Film Theory and Criticism: Introductory Readings*, 4th ed., ed. Gerald Mast, Marshall Cohen, and Leo Braudy (New York: Oxford University Press, 1992). See also Ben Singer, "Reconsidering the Classical Film Theory Canon," paper delivered at the Society for Cinema Study Conference, April 1996.

2. See Jean Mitry, *The Aesthetics and Psychology of the Cinema*, trans. Christopher King (Bloomington: Indiana University Press, 1997); Noël Carroll, *Theorizing the Moving Image* (New York: Cambridge University Press, 1996).

3. David Bordwell, "Contemporary Film Studies and the Vicissitudes of Grand Theory," in *Post-Theory: Reconstructing Film Studies*, ed. David Bordwell and Noël Carroll (Madison: University of Wisconsin Press, 1996), 3–36. In this volume, see also Noël Carroll, "Prospects for Film Theory: A Personal Assessment," 37–68. For a more sympathetic view of "post-1968" film theory, see Robert Lapsley and Michael Westlake, *Film Theory: An Introduction* (Manchester: Manchester University Press, 1988), 156–180 in particular. See also Dudley Andrew, *Concepts in Film Theory* (New York: Oxford

University Press, 1984); and Jacques Aumont, Alain Bergala, Michel Marie, and Marc Vernet, *Aesthetics of Film,* trans. and rev. Richard Neupert (Austin: University of Texas Press, 1992).

4. Bordwell and Carroll, *Post-Theory,* xiii.

5. On this, see Stefan Sharff, *The Elements of Cinema: Toward a Theory of Cinesthetic Impact* (New York: Columbia University Press, 1982), 76–83 and 137–139.

6. See Stanley Cavell, *The World Viewed: Reflections on the Ontology of Film,* enlarged ed. (Cambridge: Harvard University Press, 1979), 143.

Chapter 1: Appearance and Reality

1. See Irving Singer, *The Harmony of Nature and Spirit* (Baltimore: Johns Hopkins University Press, 1996).

2. See Hugo Münsterberg, *The Photoplay* (New York: Arno Press and The New York Times, 1970); for a discussion of Münsterberg's doctrine as well as the Myth of the Cave in Plato, see Ian Jarvie, *Philosophy of the Film: Epistemology, Ontology, Aesthetics* (New York: Routledge & Kegan Paul, 1987), 44–95 and passim. On Münsterberg, see also Carroll, "Film/Mind Analogies: The Case of Hugo Munsterberg," in *Theorizing the Moving Image,* 293–304; also 291–292.

3. Münsterberg, *The Photoplay,* 88, 95; italics deleted.

4. Ibid., 173, 220; italics deleted.

5. Ibid., 172.

6. Ibid., 150; italics deleted.

7. George Santayana, "The Photograph and the Mental Image," in *Animal Faith and Spiritual Life, Previously Unpublished and Uncollected Writings by George Santayana with Critical Essays on His Thought,* ed. John Lachs (New York: Appleton-Century-Crofts, 1967), 399–400. My discussion of Santayana includes material, now much revised,

that appears in my "Santayana and the Ontology of the Photographic Image," *The Journal of Aesthetics and Art Criticism* 36, no. 1: 39–43.

8. André Bazin, *What is Cinema?*, trans. Hugh Gray (Berkeley: University of California Press, 1967, 1971), I: 13–14. See also André Bazin, *Bazin at Work: Major Essays & Reviews from the Forties and Fifties*, trans. Alain Piette and Bert Cardullo, ed. Bert Cardullo (New York: Routledge, 1997). For important variations of Bazin's ideas, see Christian Metz, "On the Impression of Reality in the Cinema," in his *Film Language*, trans. Michael Taylor (New York: Oxford University Press, 1974), 3–15. See also Roland Barthes, "Rhetoric of the Image," in his *Image-Music-Text*, trans. Stephen Heath (Glasgow: Fontana, 1977), 32–51. For a "post-1968" critique, see Colin MacCabe, "Theory and Film: Principles of Realism and Pleasure," in his *Theoretical Essays: Film, Linguistics, Literature* (Manchester: Manchester University Press, 1985), 58–81. For a more recent, and analytic, approach, see Gregory Currie, "Film, Reality, and Illusion," in *Post-Theory*, ed. Bordwell and Carroll, 325–344. See also Joel Snyder and Neil Walsh Allen, "Photography, Vision, and Representation," *Critical Inquiry* 2, no. 1: 143–169.

9. Siegfried Kracauer, *Theory of Film: The Redemption of Physical Reality* (New York: Oxford University Press, 1965), 28.

10. On this, see Helmut Gernsheim, *Creative Photography: Aesthetic Trends* 1839–1960 (New York: Bonanza Books, 1962).

11. Bazin, *What is Cinema?*, I: 13.

12. For a discussion of Bazin's general position, see Noël Carroll, *Philosophical Problems of Classical Film Theory* (Princeton: Princeton University Press, 1988), 93–171.

13. Cavell, *The World Viewed*, 20.

14. Ibid., 23.

15. For a related criticism of Cavell's ideas, see Carroll, *Philosophical Problems of Classical Film Theory*, 144–147. For an extended discussion

of frames and borders in contrast to Cavell's, see Charles Affron, *Cinema and Sentiment* (Chicago: University of Chicago Press, 1982), 24–52. For a general critique of Cavell, see Jarvie, *Philosophy of the Film*, 95–121.

16. See Kendall Walton, "Transparent Pictures: On the Nature of Photographic Realism," *Critical Inquiry* 11, no. 2: 246–277. For a critique of Walton, see Edwin Martin, "On Seeing Walton's Great-Grandfather," followed by Walton's reply "Looking Again through Photographs," *Critical Inquiry* 12, no. 4: 796–808. See also discussion of Walton in Gregory Currie, *Image and Mind: Film, Philosophy and Cognitive Science* (Cambridge: Cambridge University Press, 1995), 50ff and passim. For a view similar to Walton's, see Roger Scruton, "Photography and Representation," *Critical Inquiry* 7, no. 3, 577–603. For critical discussion of Scruton, see Andrew, *Concepts in Film Theory*, 51–53. See also Noël Carroll's critique in "Defining the Moving Image," in *Theorizing the Moving Image*, 56–60. An earlier version of this article appears as "Towards an Ontology of the Moving Image," in *Philosophy and Film*, ed. Cynthia A. Freeland and Thomas E. Wartenberg (New York: Routledge, 1995), 68–95.

Chapter 2: *The Purple Rose of Cairo*

1. Eric Lax, "Woody Allen—Not Only a Comic," *The New York Times*, Sunday, 24 February 1985, sec. 2, pp. 1, 24; quoted in Sam G. Girgus, *The Films of Woody Allen* (Cambridge: Cambridge University Press, 1993), 70.

2. On the nature of horror as a genre in film and in literature, see Noël Carroll, *The Philosophy of Horror or Paradoxes of the Heart* (New York: Routledge, 1990), 12–58.

3. Woody Allen, *The Purple Rose of Cairo*, in *Three Films of Woody Allen* (New York: Vintage, 1987), 404. Hereafter page references appear in parentheses in the text.

4. Girgus, *The Films of Woody Allen*, 85.

5. Richard Wilbur, "Matthew VIII, 28ff.," in his *New and Collected Poems* (San Diego: Harcourt Brace Jovanovich, 1988), 154.

6. See Woody Allen, "The Kugelmass Episode," in *Side Effects* (New York: Random House, 1980), 41–55.

7. Luigi Pirandello, *Six Characters in Search of an Author,* English version by Edward Storer, in *Naked Masks,* ed. Eric Bentley (New York: E. P. Dutton, 1952), 266.

8. On the artificiality of art, see my book *The Harmony of Nature and Spirit,* particularly chaps. 6 and 7. Also see these chapters for an analysis of the concept of consummation that I use in this book.

9. Luigi Pirandello, "Preface to *Six Characters in Search of an Author,*" trans. Eric Bentley, in *Naked Masks,* 372.

10. See Girgus, *The Films of Woody Allen,* 83–84. For further discussion of *The Purple Rose of Cairo,* see Sander H. Lee, *Woody Allen's Angst: Philosophical Commentaries on His Serious Films* (Jefferson, NC: McFarland, 1997), 173–186; *Woody Allen on Woody Allen: In Conversation with Stig Björkman* (London: Faber and Faber, 1994), 148–152; Arnold W. Preussner, "Woody Allen's *The Purple Rose of Cairo* and the Genres of Comedy," in *Perspectives on Woody Allen,* ed. Renée R. Curry (New York: G. K. Hall, 1996), 91–97; Richard A. Blake, *Woody Allen: Profane and Sacred* (Lanham, MD: Scarecrow, 1995), 116–123.

Chapter 3: The Visual and the Literary

1. Erwin Panofsky, "Style and Medium in the Motion Pictures," in *Film Theory and Criticism,* ed. Mast, Cohen, and Braudy, 247.

2. Michael Roemer, "The Surfaces of Reality," in *Film: A Montage of Theories,* ed. Richard Dyer MacCann (New York: Dutton, 1966), 255–256.

3. Ibid., 259.

4. Quoted in Andrew, *The Major Film Theories,* 154.

5. George Bluestone, *Novels into Film* (Berkeley: University of California Press, 1957), 1.

6. Ibid., 20.

7. See Christian Metz, *The Imaginary Signifier: Psychoanalysis and the Cinema*, trans. Celia Britton, Annwyl Williams, Ben Brewster, and Alfred Guzzetti (Bloomington: Indiana University Press, 1982), 57–60. See also Noël Carroll, *Mystifying Movies: Fads & Fallacies in Contemporary Film Theory* (New York: Columbia University Press, 1988), 32–48, 153; Allan Casebier, *Film and Phenomenology: Toward a Realist Theory of Cinematic Representation* (Cambridge: Cambridge University Press, 1991), 112–119; and Vivian Sobchack, *The Address of the Eye: A Phenomenology of Film Experience* (Princeton: Princeton University Press, 1992), 14–32.

8. On this question, see Richard Allen, "Representation, Illusion, and the Cinema," *Cinema Journal* 32, no. 2: 21–48; and Carroll's reply in *Theorizing the Moving Image*, 366–370. Allen's paper reappears, modified, in his *Projecting Illusion: Film Spectatorship and the Impression of Reality* (Cambridge: Cambridge University Press, 1995), 81–119. See also Richard Allen, "Film Spectatorship: A Reply to Murray Smith" and Murray Smith, "Regarding Film Spectatorship: A Reply to Richard Allen," *The Journal of Aesthetics and Art Criticism* 56, no. 1: 61–65.

9. See *The Harmony of Nature and Spirit*, 120ff. I also discuss the imaginary in relation to imagination as a whole in my forthcoming book *Feeling and Imagination*. For a more sympathetic reading of Lacan, see Allen, "Althusser, Lacan, and Film Theory," in *Projecting Illusion*, 7–46, particularly 25–31.

10. Bazin, *What is Cinema?*, I: 38.

Chapter 4: *Death in Venice*

A shorter and now much revised version of this chapter appears in my "*Death in Venice:* Visconti and Mann," *MLN* 91, no. 6, 1348–1359.

1. Thomas Mann, *Death in Venice and Seven Other Stories*, trans. H. T. Lowe-Porter (New York: Vintage Books, 1954), 50.

2. Thomas Mann, *Death in Venice*, trans. Kenneth Burke (New York: Modern Library, 1970), 66. All other quotations in this chapter are taken from the Lowe-Porter translation; page citations appear in the text in parentheses.

3. For speculation about this, see Ronald Hayman, *Thomas Mann: A Biography* (New York: Scribner, 1995), 258.

4. It is worth noting, however, that in an early interview Visconti characterized his theme in this film as "love without eroticism, without sexuality." (Quoted in Geoffrey Wagner, *The Novel and the Cinema* [Rutherford, NJ: Fairleigh Dickinson University Press, 1975], 343.) But in another interview Visconti describes the theme very differently, saying: "Certain goals are reachable only through Eros." (Quoted in Lietta Tornabuoni, "Visconti tra Mann e Proust," *La Stampa*, 3 March 1970.) On this, see Claretta Tonetti, *Luchino Visconti* (Boston: Twayne, 1983), 142–148. See also Lino Miccichè, *"Morte a Venezia" di Luchino Visconti* (Bologna: Cappelli, 1971). For critical comment on Visconti's use of erotic themes and his "mishandling of cinematic language," see Elaine Mancini, *Luchino Visconti: A Guide to References and Resources* (Boston: G. K. Hall, 1986), 22. For further discussion, see Henry Bacon, *Visconti: Explorations of Beauty and Decay* (Cambridge: Cambridge University Press, 1998), 155–172.

5. At this point, Katherine Stern comments: "My sense is that the barber's attentions unmistakably evoke embalming in Mann's version: remember that Aschenbach is 'enveloped in a white sheet,' like a corpse. . . . Moreover, I would argue that the man in make-up is a recognizable figure of 'decadence,' always associated with sadness and death, and that Mann fully intends us to visualize Aschenbach's feminized, clownish visage and to be alarmed by its portents" (Personal communication).

Chapter 5: Communication and Alienation

1. For a more recent suggestion that photography is a "minor art," see Virgil C. Aldrich, *Philosophy of Art* (Englewood Cliffs, NJ: Prentice-Hall, 1963), 62.

2. Bazin, *What is Cinema?*, I: 12.

3. Similar ideas figure prominently in the writings of both Bazin and Metz. In "Reconsidering the Classical Film Theory Canon," cited above, Ben Singer quotes the following from a 1924 article by Iris Barry in *The Adelphi*: "I often consider, when I am in the cinema, how much each unique individual sitting in the darkness there, watching that representation of other individuals interacting on the screen, resembles the solitary creatures who sit at home behind a veil of window-curtains, peeping out at passers-by. There is the same isolation, the same attention. There is something of the same need."

4. F. E. Sparshott, "Basic Film Aesthetics," in *Film Theory and Criticism: Introductory Readings,* ed. Gerald Mast and Marshall Cohen (New York: Oxford University Press, 1974), 216–217.

5. Jean Mitry, *Esthétique et psychologie du cinéma* (Paris: Editions universitaires, 1963), I: 179. My translation. In Mitry, *The Aesthetics and Psychology of the Cinema*, 80.

6. Walter Benjamin, "The Work of Art in the Age of Mechanical Reproduction," in *Illuminations* (New York: Harcourt, Brace & World, 1968), 226.

7. See *Acting in Film, with Michael Caine,* BBC TV, 1987. See also Michael Caine, *Acting in Film: An Actor's Take on Movie Making* (New York: Applause Theatre Book, 1990), 3–6.

8. In *Feeling and Imagination* I distinguish between alienation, detachment, and estrangement in a way that augments the present argument.

9. Benjamin, *Illuminations*, 236.

Chapter 6: *The Rules of the Game*

1. *Rules of the Game: A Film by Jean Renoir*, trans. John McGrath and Maureen Teitelbaum (New York: Simon & Schuster, 1970), 102. Hereafter page references appear in parentheses in the text.

2. See Irving Singer, *The Goals of Human Sexuality* (New York: Norton, 1973), 41–65.

3. See Irving Singer, *Mozart and Beethoven: The Concept of Love in Their Operas* (Baltimore: Johns Hopkins University Press, 1977).

4. In the American videotape, the card states: "This story, set on the eve of World War II, is intended as entertainment—not as social criticism."

5. Gerald Mast, *The Comic Mind: Comedy and the Movies*, 2d ed. (Chicago: University of Chicago Press, 1979), 6.

6. Jean Renoir, *My Life and My Films*, trans. Norman Denny (New York: Atheneum, 1974), 172.

7. See Jean Renoir, *Renoir My Father* (Boston: Little, Brown, 1962).

8. For illustrations of Coco's bust, see Paul Haesaerts, *Renoir Sculptor* (New York: Reynal and Hitchcock, 1947), 16, plate IV, and 30, plate XXXVI.

9. See Jean Renoir, "An Early Scenario for *The Rules of the Game* (extracts)," in André Bazin, *Jean Renoir*, ed. François Truffaut, trans. W. W. Halsey II and William H. Simon (New York: Simon and Schuster, 1973), 187–197.

10. For further discussion of many of the points in this chapter, see Alexander Sesonske's thorough examination of *The Rules of the Game* in *Jean Renoir: The French Films 1924–1939* (Cambridge: Harvard University Press, 1980), 378–440. See also Leo Braudy, *Jean Renoir: The World of His Films* (Garden City: Doubleday, 1972); Gerald Mast, *Filmguide to* The Rules of the Game (Bloomington: Indiana University Press, 1973); Raymond Durgnat, *Jean Renoir* (Berkeley: Univer-

sity of California Press, 1974); Penelope Gilliatt, *Jean Renoir* (New York: McGraw-Hill, 1975); Jean Renoir, *Renoir on Renoir*, trans. Carol Volk (Cambridge: Cambridge University Press, 1990); and Cavell, *The World Viewed*, 219–231.

Conclusion: Cinematic Transformation

1. Panofsky, "Style and Medium in the Motion Pictures," 237.

2. On this, see Harry Geduld, *Filmguide to* Henry V (Bloomington: Indiana University Press, 1973), 19. See also Dudley Andrew, "Realism, Rhetoric, and the Painting of History in *Henry V*," in *Film in the Aura of Art* (Princeton: Princeton University Press, 1984), 131–151.

3. *Laurence Olivier: A Life*, television documentary (London: South Bank Show, 17 October 1982).

4. See my book *Mozart and Beethoven*, 3–23.

Index